Employment Protection and Unemployment

European University Studies

Europäische Hochschulschriften

Publications Universitaires Européennes

Series V

Economics and Management

Reihe V Série V

Volks- und Betriebswirtschaft

Sciences économiques, gestion d'entreprise

Vol./Bd. 3246

PETER LANG

Frankfurt am Main · Berlin · Bern · Bruxelles · New York · Oxford · Wien

Nikolai Stähler

Employment Protection and Unemployment

A Theoretical Analysis Evaluating Recent Policy Proposals

PETER LANG
Europäischer Verlag der Wissenschaften

Bibliographic Information published by the Deutsche Nationalbibliothek
The Deutsche Nationalbibliothek lists this publication in the Deutsche Nationalbibliografie; detailed bibliographic data is available in the internet at <http://www.d-nb.de>.

Zugl.: Mainz, Univ., Diss., 2006

D 77
ISSN 0531-7339
ISBN-10: 3-631-55947-X
ISBN-13: 978-3-631-55947-5
US-ISBN 0-8204-8764-3

www.peterlang.de

To Verena

Acknowledgements

The present book was accepted as my PhD-thesis at the Johannes Gutenberg-University of Mainz on August 25, 2006. It was accomplished during the time period starting May 2003 until February 2006, when I got the much appreciated opportunity to work as a research assistant at the Institute of Economic Policy.

I am particulary indebted to Prof. Dr. Laszlo Goerke, my supervisor and the chair of the Institute of Economic Policy, for his advice and tuition. He found the right combination of the carrot and the stick to make me work hard enough to complete this thesis and having fun while doing so. It was also a very good experience working in his team. Anyone writing a PhD-thesis would certainly be happy to have someone like Laszlo Goerke as supervisor. I would also like to thank Prof. Dr. Martin Kolmar who was the second member of my thesis committee and initiated the so-called Goerke-Kolmar-Seminar where I received a lot of helpful comments. Also, many thanks to Prof. Dr. Beatrice Weder di Mauro for being the third member of my thesis committee.

It was a lot of help and fun to be member of the research group '*Heterogenous Labor: Positive and Normative Aspects of the Skill Structure of Labor*' founded by the German Research Foundation (DFG). Thanks to everyone there. The regular meetings were always very fruitful. The opportunity given by the membership in the research group to travel and present my work at different conferences additionally helped a lot to improve this work. All the financial support of the DFG is gratefully acknowledged.

A lot of this thesis was in circulation in several papers and was discussed by several people face-to-face. I am very much indebted to Florian Baumann for always finding the time to read my papers and for the intense discussions. Without his help, this thesis would certainly look a lot different. Special thanks to Salvatore Barbaro and Magnus Hoffmann not only for their help with LaTeX. Bernd Bracht, Sven Drebes, Tim Friehe,

Frank Hochapfel, Marcus Jansen, Jörg Lingens, Thomas Mohr, Christoph Moser, Thorsten Nestmann, Matthias Oschinski, Dorothee Schmidt, Jan Schumacher, Dana Sisak, Sascha Thielmann, Prof. Dr. Georg Tillmann and Michael Wedow who were especially persistent in questioning my basic assumptions, challenging my conclusions, and forcing me to re-think what I was doing. It was a lot of fun having you around. I also thank Martin Glimm, Rolf Helmes, Christian Oberpriller, Thomas Schneider and Markus Seibold for very good and helpful discussions and the encouragement during times of disappointment. The introduction to the "cosmos of university" and how things work there by Alexandra Lehmann was very helpful. Thanks to Daniel Scott for proofreading this book. Not being an economist, it must have been a lot of fun!

Thanks a lot to my family, Ingrid, Eberhard and Kathrin Stähler, Claudia Durm-Weggenmann and Karl and Carmen Weggenmann for giving me the opportunity to study economics and for the huge amount of support and encouragement during the time I was working on this thesis. I hope that you know how much I appreciate all you have done for me.

Last, but certainly not least, I want to thank Verena Weggenmann for sharing her life with me and being there when I needed her most. Without her, I would not be what I am now. This book is dedicated to her.

In writing a thesis, one accumulates a long list of debts. I appologise to anyone who has been inadvertently left out.

Nikolai Stähler, Mainz-Kastel, November 2006

Contents

List of Figures

List of Tables

Chapter 1

Introduction

"It is the orthodox view that the persistence of high unemployment is explained by the rigidities imposed by labor market institutions such as centralized collective bargaining, (...), employment protection laws, and unemployment benefits." (Howell and Huebler 2005, p. 35). By this quotation, it becomes evident that economists have several widely accepted explanations for the phenomena of unemployment (for an overview, see also Blanchard 2006). While many economists belief that only a thorough across-the-board reform will successfully yield a sustained reduction of unemployment (e.g., Coe and Snower 1997), others are of the opinion that one should rather single out separate institutions that are particularly harmful to employment and one should concentrate reformation efforts on these institutions (e.g., Layard and Nickell 1999). Lately, the discussion about employment protection has attracted disproportionately high attention. We can find several reasons for this attraction. Strong employment protection is often claimed to be the cause for persistently high long-term unemployment (see, e.g., Canziani and Petrolongo 2001). Employment protection exists in nearly every developed country, albeit the strictness differs, of course. In public debates, high employment protection is claimed to serve social justice for employees, assumed to be the weaker market side on the labour market, as it increases the workers' job and income security (OECD 2004a, p. 61). In contrast to this allegedly positive effect, employers face limited labour adjustment possibilities (equivalent to higher labour adjustment costs) through dismissal protection. But the most important reason for the high scientific interest in employment protection certainly is that its effects on unemployment are still ambiguous, both from a theoretical and an empirical point of view (see be-

low a brief description of the most recent literature, a more detailed overview is given in chapter 3). In this work, we concentrate our attention on the effects of employment protection on unemployment. However, the analysis of those effects is embedded into different institutional frameworks. Hence, we follow both Coe and Snower (1997) and Layard and Nickel (1999) by combining the fact that it seems to be important to analyse isolated effects of a single labour market institution (namely, employment protection), but still bear in mind that the effects might differ when connected to different labour market institutions such as unemployment insurance and different bargaining structures. As, e.g., Blau and Kahn (1999) or Agell (2002) have already shown, we also find that the institutional framework matters.

Therefore, we focus our attention on the effects of employment protection on unemployment in different institutional settings. The reason for choosing the four aspects described below is motivated by the fact that they have gained prominence in recent policy debate in continental Europe. Our analysis is mainly a positive one, characterising and describing the effects that occur. Normative aspects are only briefly sketched. The aspects chosen are, first, the analysis of an experienced rated unemployment insurance. Second, the effects of pure firing costs and severance payments in the presence of judicial mistakes. Third, we highlight the effects of employment protection on ex-ante skill formation of workers and the resulting unemployment effects. Finally, we consider the interactions of employment protection and collective bargaining (beneath and in the corresponding chapters, a more detailed explanation of these aspects is given).

Theoretical economic literature about labour market analysis has gone through different stages. First approaches explaining labour market developments are done in basic static models mainly concentrating on labour demand and labour supply with perfect and complete markets, as found in every standard textbook about economics (see, e.g., Pindyck and Rubinfeld 2005). This labour market is referred to as the Walrasian labour market. Firms' demand for labour is achieved by standard profit maximisation with respect to labour, and workers' labour supply is either exogenously given or derived by workers' utility maximisation with respect to a certain consumption-leisure decision. The price of labour (wages) is then determined by the labour demand and labour supply function. Only rigidities due to imperfect markets can cause involuntary unemployment. It seems obvious that in static models, employment protection only increases labour costs and therefore reduces employment. Evidently, other model types incorporating involuntary unemployment, employment flows and endogenous reasons for job creation and job destruction need to be consulted for an analysis of employment protection rules to make sense. There are mainly three types of models that have become accepted in economic literature: the "union model", the "efficiency wage model" and the "search and matching model".

In union models, the wage rigidity which produces unemployment results because unions set wages that exceed the wage resulting in perfect markets. This is due to the fact that unions tend to maximise the utility of their employed members. Even when unions take into consideration the utility of unemployed workers, this result applies. First approaches to introduce unions into labour market models can be found in Dunlop (1944), Fellner (1947), and Cartter (1959). In their models, a single union sets wages which firms then take as given when determining their optimal employment level. This is called the "monopoly union model". Those models were extended by a regime where firms and (single or firm-specific) unions bargain over wages, the so called "right-to-manage model", or where unions and firms bargain over wages and employment simultaneously, the "efficient bargaining model", first found in Leontief (1946). Under the latter wage bargaining structure, unions and firms tend to be better off than in the "right-to-manage regime" as none of the parties forces the other to accept wages or employment levels and both parties participate in the decision process (see, e.g., McDonald and Solow 1981 or Booth 1995a). Even though these models generate involuntary unemployment, they mostly lack a dynamic process that generates employment flows which is an essential condition when discussing dismissal protection. For union models, this problem has been addressed by Booth (1995b) and Belot and van Ours (2004) in a fairly artificial way. They assume that firms already employ a certain stock of workers and introduce a probability that some workers get hit by a shock and become redundant. Firms face dismissal costs in the case where they lay off employees due to such a shock. A more sophisticated process is described by Modesto and Thomas (2001) who integrate an infinite time horizon or Modesto (2004) who uses an overlapping-generations-framework. Nevertheless, employment protection has hardly been discussed in union models so far.

Efficiency wage models are based on the realisation in development economics that job performance increases with increasing nutrition (see Leibenstein 1957 or Bliss and Stern 1978). The assumption that job productivity is a function of nutrition is the basis for the labour market model of Stiglitz (1976). For underdeveloped countries, an excess labour supply accompanied by an efficiency wage exceeding the level of subsistence can be explained with this theory. The efficiency wage hypothesis has soon be transformed to the "shirking model" of Shapiro and Stiglitz (1984) for developed countries. As nutrition does not play such a fundamentally important role in developed countries, the argument made in "shirking models" is that workers tend to provide less working effort than is expected by the employer which is, due to asymmetric information, only imperfectly observable by firms. If workers are caught shirking, they are dismissed. A high enough efficiency wage prevents the worker from shirking, because of the expected utility loss. Due to the efficiency wage, which exceeds the equivalent wage resulting in complete and perfect markets, involuntary unemployment results. Exogenous shocks may cause the firm to lay off workers or hire new ones which generates employment flows. This gives room to introduce employment protection, as there exists involuntary unemployment and dismissal probabilities. Well-known papers integrating employment protection into efficiency wage models are by Fella (2000) or Goerke (2002b). They find that severance payments reduce the workers' wage claim and may have positive effects on employment under certain circumstances.

Search and matching models assume that unemployment exists because of search frictions in an economy. It is considered that job seeking is costly and takes time for both workers and firms. This type of model results from the dynamic macroeconomic theory. A good overview about the basis of the development of this model type can be found in Ljungqvist and Sargent (2000). In matching models, unemployment and vacancies exist at the same time and, therefore, the probabilities of a vacancy being filled and of an unemployed worker finding a job are determined endogenously. Additionally, endogenous job destruction has been introduced (see, e.g., Mortensen and Pissarides 1994 or Pissarides 2000 for an overview). Therefore, matching models seem ideal when discussing employment effects of dismissal protection, as they incorporate involuntary unemployment, endogenous job creation and job destruction as well as employment flows. A further advantage of search and matching models is that the above mentioned model types, namely, union models and efficiency wage models, can be included into the matching framework, as has been shown by Mortensen and Pissarides (1999). Recent works combining employment protection and matching models are by Garibaldi (1998) and Mortensen and Pissarides (1999). Because matching models can incorporate employment flows, involuntary unemployment and different wage bargaining structures, our theoretical analysis is based on this type of model. Chapter 3 gives a more detailed overview of the development of research in this model type.

The main findings of economic literature about employment protection can be summarised as follows. Employment protection decreases the probabilities of dismissals, as each lay-off is accompanied by some additional cost. At the same time, it decreases the incentive for job creation, as employers, in their decision whether to hire a new worker, will take into account the likelihood that firing costs will be incurred in the future. Therefore, the overall effect of employment protection on unemployment is ambiguous from a theoretical point of view (see, e.g., Bertola 1990, Garibaldi 1998, or Mortensen and Pissarides 1999, just to mention a few). Empirical analyses confirm these ambiguous effects and has not yet been able to find a clearly positive nor negative link between employment protection and unemployment (see Addison and Teixeira 2003, Baker et al. 2004, Blanchard and Portugal 2001, Heckman and Pagés 2000 and OECD 2004a).[1] As already mentioned above, the following analysis concentrates on four aspects of dismissal protection that have gained prominence lately in both, political and scientific discussions. The following gives a brief description of what we will be analysing. A more specific overview of recent literature and the effects at work is then presented in the corresponding chapters.

An experience rated unemployment insurance exists in the United States, while it does not in most continental European countries (Anderson and Meyer 2000).[2] However, the introduction of such a system is being discussed in Europe (see European Commission 2004). Also, the German Council of Economic Experts has demanded an experience rated unemployment insurance for Germany (German Council of Economic Experts 2003). In most European countries, unemployment benefits are financed with contributions of employed workers or of employers. This gives rise to an externality as these contributions increase the firms' labour costs (because they have to pay this contribution per employed worker). If only employed workers participate in financing the system, an individually efficient dismissal from the firm's point of view creates additional costs for other firms and might, therefore, be socially inefficient for the entire economy. This is because as soon as a worker is laid off, the financial requirements of the unemployment insurance increase, while the number of contributors to finance unemployment benefits decreases. According to our analysis, dismissal taxes make the firm consider the social costs caused by firing a worker, and the externality can be resolved. At first sight, dismissal taxes increase firms' tax burden. But, firstly, an increase in dismissal taxes allows a decrease in contributions

[1] A more detailed description of the literature about employment protection is found in chapter 3.

[2] There are some exceptions. In France, firms that lay off workers above the age of 50 have to pay part of the unemployment benefits through the Delalande tax, for example. Nevertheless, experience rated unemployment insurance is rare in continental Europe as can easily be confirmed by Behaghel et al. (2005).

that have to be paid by the worker. Secondly, there being fewer dismissals decreases the financial need of the unemployment insurance, which additionally reduces the contributions to the unemployment insurance. So in total, firms face a smaller tax burden under certain conditions, which raises the incentive for job creation. Thus, due to fewer dismissals and more job creation, unemployment unambiguously falls in a system with experience rated unemployment insurance. Similar results are obtained by Cahuc and Malherbet (2004) and Fath and Fuest (2005a, 2005c). A more detailed description and the analysis are found in chapter 4.

Severance payments, in contrast to pure firing costs, generate a payoff for the worker in the case of a dismissal. The worker anticipates this payment and, therefore, may accept lower wages as he is compensated for the risk of being dismissed. Lower wages create the incentive for more job creation. This "advantage" of severance payments over firing costs has already been found in the well-known paper of Lazear (1990). For Germany, again the German Council of Economic Experts suggests reducing pure dismissal costs and increasing the level of severance payments to be paid in the case of a dismissal due to these reasons (German Council of Economic Experts 2005, 2006). It has to be considered, though, that in most countries, only those workers who are laid off due to operational reasons are entitled to a severance payment. Workers fired because of disciplinary or personal reasons are not. If the reason for the dismissal is not perfectly verifiable, a conflict results between workers and firms which is usually settled in court (see, e.g., OECD 2004a). Judges might make mistakes in the reviewing process. Galdón-Sánches and Güell (2003) show that in the presence of judicial mistakes, an increase of the level of severance payments decreases employment. This is the opposite of what has been found by Lazear (1990), Fella (2000) or Goerke (2002b), for example. Following up on the analysis by Galdón-Sánches and Güell (2003), we present a model with severance payments and judicial mistakes. While Galdón-Sánches and Güell (2003) present a model with exogenous dismissal decision, we present a model where the layoff decision of firms is endogenised. We find that high judicial mistakes themselves increase unemployment. Further, we are able to show that for small judicial mistakes, an increase of the level of severance payments decreases unemployment, while the opposite holds for large errors. There is a threshold for the magnitude of the judicial mistakes that turns the "advantage" of severance payments over pure firing costs into a "disadvantage". The analysis is to be found in chapter 5.

Publicly, it is often claimed that the comparative advantage of the developed world can only be kept through a high level of education within these countries. Taking this argument, we analyse which effects employment protection has on the ex-ante decision of workers to obtain education. Dismissal costs seem to influence education obtained "on-the-job", as has been shown by Burda (2003), Fella (2005) and Wasmer (2003). On the one hand, firms tend to invest less in training activities due to more employment protection, since higher firing costs can be compensated by lowering education costs (see, e.g., Burda 2003, Fella 2005, or Wasmer 2003). On the other hand, higher job security raises workers' incentives to contribute to the firm in form of training activities (see Bean 1997, Fella 2005, Südekum and Rühmann 2003 and Wasmer 2003). Hence, employment protection influences the labour market outcome and education. However, a huge part of an individual skill formation takes place before entering the labour market (OECD 2004b). Empirical data finds that countries with a high degree of employment protection tend to have an above average percentage of population with high education. Further, it has already been demonstrated that highly skilled workers face shorter unemployment duration and lower dismissal probabilities (OECD 2004a). This evokes the question whether employment protection affects the ex-ante education decision of workers. We show that if workers obtain a sufficiently large fraction of the rent created by skill formation, higher employment protection increases the incentive to get educated. The effect on the unemployment rate is ambiguous because higher employment protection still decreases the firms' incentive for job creation (see chapter 6 for a detailed analysis).

As the models presented above mainly picture an Anglo-Saxon labour market structure, where firms and workers bargain more or less individually over wages, we also introduce a more continental European point of view into the analysis. Unionisation is one of the characteristics of European labour markets (OECD 2004a). So far, unions have been introduced into matching models by Mortensen and Pissarides (1999) or Garibaldi and Violante (2005). They consider unions that only represent employed workers. Firms take wages set by the union as given according to the "monopoly union" approach (Booth 1995a). We consider "large" firms that employ more than one worker in matching models and firm-specific unions that take the utility of their employed members as well as the utility of all unemployed workers into consideration. The union wage depends positively on the re-employment probability of unemployed workers and the dismissal probability of employed workers. It negatively depends on the level of employment. An increase of employment protection raises the individual firm's expected labour costs and forces the firm to reduce employment. The reduction of employment yields lower re-employment probabilities for unemployed workers in equilibrium, which decreases the unions' wage claim on the one hand. On the other hand, less employment increases the union wage. Whether the total wage effect is positive or negative cannot be said from a theoretical point of view. But even if the union wage claim falls, the wage reduction cannot overcompensate the additional expected labour costs resulting from an increase of employment protection. Therefore, unemployment unambiguously increases in a unionised economy. The model presented can be understood as a first step of how to integrate large firms, unions and employment protection into matching models. Further research in this direction is certainly needed. The corresponding analysis is in chapter 7.

The work is organized as follows. In chapter 2, employment protection legislations are briefly described. Chapter 3 provides an overview of the literature of employment protection in search and matching models. Chapter 4 analyses the effects of "experience rating". In chapter 5, the implications of severance payments and judicial mistakes are addressed. Chapter 6 shows which effects employment protection has on the incentive for ex-ante skill formation. In chapter 7, we concentrate on the effects of dismissal protection in combination with a unionised wage bargaining structure. The main findings are summarized in chapter 8. A mathematical appendix is added.

Chapter 2

Different Dimensions of Employment Protection

Before starting the following theoretical analysis, it seems appropriate to say some words about what employment protection actually is and how it is modelled. Therefore, this chapter briefly defines employment protection and its dimensions, in the tighter and in the broader sense. Further, we explain how employment protection is integrated into the theoretical framework and point out a possible weakness of this way of integration. Section 2.2 gives an overview of the most important regulations in Germany. It should not be misinterpreted as a full judicial review of the legislative system in Germany. It is, rather, a short outline of those regulations which we are concerned with.

2.1 Theoretical Foundations and the OECD Indicator

We consider dismissal protection to be a microeconomic (or individual) measure for job security which is institutionally determined according to Walwei (1996), i.e., "*explicit or implicit rules and provisions putting a restraint on the ability of firms to dismiss workers*" (see Büchtemann 1993, p. 8).[1] With this definition of employment protection, dismissal protection is

[1]This definition is more or less equivalent to Pissarides (2001, p. 136) who claims employment protection to be "... *any set of regulations, either legislated or written, that limit employer's ability to dismiss the worker without delay or cost.*"

considered to explicitly and only influence the employees' job security with their current employer. Further, dismissal protection should not be equated with a full protection against job loss. In fact, employment protection refers to rules and regulations that protect employees against (unfair) layoffs and also includes rules and regulations for just dismissals (as we will see below, this can, e.g., include notice periods, severance payments, etc.).

The definitions presented below follow Grubb and Wells (1993). In principle, these definitions have become commonly accepted and used by the OECD to calculate the country-specific strictness of employment protection (see, e.g., Di Tella and MacCulloch 2005, OECD 1999 or OECD 2004a). Employment protection in the tighter sense refers to the regulations that have to be fulfilled for individually just dismissals of regularly employed workers. Dismissal protection can be differentiated into three categories: procedural requirements, notice periods and severance payments and difficulties for employers.

Procedural requirements include legal procedures which have to be maintained when dismissing a worker that can retard the dismissal. Examples of such legal procedures are admonitions, the duty to inform or consult a third party (e.g., the workers' council) and possibly the affirmation of such a third party.

Notice periods and severance payments for layoffs through no fault of the worker determine how long a dismissal must be announced before it can be enforced and how much compensation a worker gets for the job loss. Usually, notice periods and the amount of severance payments increase with the employees' job tenure.

The category difficulties for employers adverts to the legal definition of just and unjust dismissals (including regulations of what are appropriate efforts to avoid layoffs or potentially social plans) and to the consequences of what happens in cases of unjust dismissals (including compensation and possibly re-hiring). Besides that, this category also includes regulations about probation periods, as laying off a worker is usually easier during those periods. Next to the regulations of individual dismissals, there are additional requirements that have to be fulfilled in the case of mass redundancies in many countries. Those requirements include the legal definition of a mass redundancy, the obligation for communication and negotiation with labour representatives and/or with the corresponding authorities, and, if applicable, additional respites, additional selection criteria of whom to dismiss, and additional severance payments in the case that those exceed the ones of individual dismissals.

Employment protection in the broader sense includes regulations about temporary employment, such as acceptance, maximal number of successive contracts for the same post and maximal cumulative duration of temporary work. Also, legal working time and rules about the flexibility of working time can be interpreted in such a way. In the following analysis, we concentrate on employment protection in the tighter sense, as we do not focus our attention on temporary but on regular work. However, we should note that L'Haridon and Malherbet (2003) show for French data that short-term contracts might have bigger effects on unemployment than pure firing costs.

The dimensions of employment protection derived by Grubb and Wells (1993) are used by the OECD to calculate an indicator measuring the strictness of employment protection in each country, the so-called "EPL Strictness Indicator" (OECD 1999, 2004a). The OECD uses the categories and sub-categories mentioned above. After reviewing the legal regulations in each countries, the OECD scores the strictness for each category and sub-category, ranging from 0 (no protection) up to 6 (very high protection), depending on the category the score was set for. The higher the score is, the stricter is employment protection in the corresponding country. After evaluating the scores for the strictness of each category and sub-category, the index is calculated by weighting each category with its assumed importance. In table 2.1, the strictness of employment protection for regular dismissals of selected countries is shown for the year 2003 (taken from the most recent OECD report (OECD 2004a)).[2]

From table 2.1, we can confirm the common view that the Anglo-Saxon countries tend to have lower employment protection than the continental European ones. Nevertheless, even the continental European countries differ significantly in the strictness in each category, even though their overall strictness of employment protection seems to be similar. In the following analysis, employment protection is mainly modelled as some exogenous firing costs that have to be paid to some third party when firms lay off a worker (unless it is directly specified differently as, e.g., a severance payment). All dimensions mentioned above are included in this exogenous dismissal cost which more or less represents the overall strictness of employment protection. Evidently, this is a quite simplifying assumption. Hence, the modelling could be driving the results. It would, for example, be possible that the regulations determining the difficulty to dismiss a worker are more relevant for the firms hiring and firing decisions than procedural inconveniences (or vice

[2] A detailed explanation of the EPL Strictness Indicator can be found in OECD (2004a), pp. 107 to 125. It should be noted that Bertola et al. (2000) point out that an adequate estimation of the strictness of employment protection according to the above described criteria might be only fragmentary and misleading.

Country	Procedural Incon-veniences	Notice Periods & Severance Payments	Difficulty of Dismissal	Overall Strict-ness
Australia	1.5	1.0	2.0	1.5
France	2.8	1.9	3.0	2.5
Germany	3.5	1.3	3.3	2.7
Norway	2.0	1.0	3.8	2.3
United Kingdom	1.0	1.1	1.3	1.1
United States	0.0	0.0	0.5	0.2

Table 2.1: EPL Strictness for Regular Dismissals

versa). Then, assuming a similar level of employment protection for France, Germany and Norway might not be appropriate, because while the difficulties of dismissals in Norway are about one point higher than in France, the opposite holds for procedural inconveniences. Nevertheless, the modelling of employment protection as exogenously given firing costs has become an accepted way to integrate employment protection into theoretical economic models (see, e.g., Mortensen and Pissarides 1999).

2.2 The Case of Germany

Basically, employment protection in Germany is regulated by law in the *Bürgerliches Gesetzbuch* (BGB) and, more specifically, in the *Kündigungsschutzgesetz* (KSchG). General employment protection applies for firms with more than five full-time employed workers (§ 23 KSchG).[3]

Starting with the last category presented above, difficulties of dismissals, we see that according to § 1 KSchG, layoffs can only be effectively declared if there exist justifiable reasons. Such reasons can be found in the person of the worker (personal dismissals), the behaviour of the worker (disciplinary dismissals) or in the economic situation of the firm (operational

[3]Burgert (2006) conducts a more detailed empirical analysis about the implications of such a threshold on job creation in Germany. He finds - in contrast to the claim made by many officials - that there seems to be no significant evidence that the threshold hinders small firms to expand in economically favourable times.

dismissals). It is difficult to give a universally valid classification of personal or disciplinary reasons. Personal reasons generally involve a substantial and durable derogation of the firm's interest due to a lack of ability of the worker himself (due to, e.g., illness, age, applicability, matter of conscience), while disciplinary reasons require a considerable, durable and repeatable violation of the employment contract by the worker (usually on purpose, as, e.g., stealing, abuse of company properties, etc.). For personal dismissals, the employer must prove that there is no alternative job available for the corresponding worker within the firm. It is of the court's decision whether the conditions for personal or disciplinary layoffs are fulfilled.[4] Operational dismissal reasons are easier to handle as this is an entrepreneurial decision. However, it is not possible to fire a certain worker due to operational reasons and employ another one for the same post right after the dismissal (§ 1 KSchG). In those cases where a worker finds his dismissal to be unjustifiable, each worker has the right for a judicial review according to § 4 KSchG. The employer faces the burden of proof for the dismissal to be fair. If the layoff is then declared to be unfair, the employee has the right to be re-hired according to § 9 KSchG. As in most cases, re-hiring is not a desirable option, neither for the worker, nor for the employer, § 9 KSchG includes the possibility of a contract termination accompanied with a severance payment that has to be paid to the employee. The contract termination needs the approval of the worker. The court determines the extend of the severance payment according to §§ 9 and 10 KSchG. As a reference value, a worker is entitled to receive half a monthly gross wage per year of employment within the corresponding firm (see also § 1a KSchG). Of course, actual severance payments can exceed this reference value. During the year 2001, 27% of the dismissals were brought to court in Germany (German Council of Economic Experts 2003).

Procedural inconveniences include that employers must give their employees a dissuasion, also for personal and disciplinary dismissals as workers might not know that their abilities or actions interfere with the firm's interests. Further to the above mentioned, in Germany, operational layoffs must be socially fair (§ 112 *Betriebsverfassungsgesetz* (BetrVG)). Social fairness means that the dismissal follows a redundancy plan complying with § 1(3) KSchG. Through the redundancy plan, firms are forced to dismiss those workers with the least seniority first, take the workers' personal situation

[4]The German Federal Labour Court, Bundesarbeitsgericht (BAG), sentences to § 1 KSchG from May 20th, 1988 (AP 9) and from January 26th, 1995 (AP 34) give some judgment guidelines of German case law. Nevertheless, those dismissals involve some insecurity from the employers' point of view.

into consideration (e.g., if the worker is single, has family, debts, etc.) and, the redundancy plan dictates that workers' council members are to be fired last. Additionally, the workers' council has the right to be heard in the case of a redundancy (§ 102 BetrVG), even though their influence on the decision is limited.

Legal notice periods are regulated by § 622 BGB. Generally, the employment relationship can be canceled with a notice period of four weeks to the 15th or the end of a month. But the time increases with increasing job tenure. For a worker employed at a firm for 20 years or more, legal notice periods can go up to seven months (§ 622(2) BGB). It has to be mentioned, though, that in most collective labour agreements, notice periods are extended and, therefore, legal notice periods only apply for some workers.[5] A payment of severance payments is not legally determined, with the exception of a dismissal declared unfair as already mentioned above. Nevertheless, cancellation agreements between workers and firms, regulated in § 623 BGB, usually include severance payments.

Mass redundancies are regulated in § 17 KSchG and can only be effective in agreement with the corresponding federal employment office (§ 18 KSchG). In principle, the above described premises also apply, while the importance of social plans is fortified. Further, a lot of rules and regulations which protect different groups of people, as, e.g., families through maternal protection (regulated in § 9(3) *Mutterschutzgesetz* (MuSchG)), disabled people (regulated in § 85 *Sozialgesetzbuch* (SGB) IX), etc., exist. As this work concentrates on general individual employment protection, we will not focus on those specific issues. A more detailed description of the employment protection legislation in Germany can be found in Hromadka and Maschmann (2002).

[5]About 70% of the employed workers are bounded by collective labour agreements (see, e.g., Ellguth and Kohaut 2005).

Chapter 3

Developments of Literature

This chapter gives an overview of the development and findings of recent economic literature about employment protection. The main focus is on search and matching models as these are the basis for our theoretical analysis. However, we incorporate other strands of literature to highlight the differences or similarities of the results. First, we briefly sketch the conventional findings of theoretical literature on employment protection in various model frameworks. Then, we describe the development of the Mortensen and Pissarides (1994) type matching model, as this has become the most accepted when analysing labour markets and the implications of policy instruments on labour market outcomes. We shortly describe the efficiency implications of this model type and point out the effects of different policy instruments that have been introduced. Then, we give a detailed overview of the literature on employment protection in matching models.

Theoretical research into the effects of dismissal regulations mostly concentrates on two different ways of modelling employment protection, namely pure firing costs and severance payments.[1] Pure firing costs are paid to some exogenous party, representing those costs that relate to all legal regulations delaying the dismissal, such as, e.g., notice periods, procedural requirements, etc. (as seen in chapter 2). Severance payments represent

[1]Exceptions are amongst others Garibaldi (1998)'s modelling employment protection as administrative barriers or Pissarides (2001), who explicitly models employment protection as notice periods rather than general firing costs. However, their results are equivalent to those of pure firing costs.

transfers to workers that have been dismissed. Pure firing costs yield ambiguous effects on unemployment due to less job destruction and less job creation, as already mentioned in chapter 1. These ambiguous effects of dismissal costs on unemployment have already been demonstrated by Bertola (1990, 1992) or Bentolila and Bertola (1990) in models with exogenously given wages. In contrast, Lazear (1990) or Fella (2000) find in an efficiency model that the employment effect is neutral or can be even positive when employment protection is modelled as a pure severance payment. This is due to the fact that workers claim high wages to be compensated for the risk of losing their job. Severance payment reduces their wage claim, which leaves the firms' employment decision unchanged or even gives them an incentive to hire more workers if the severance payment is set the right way. Finding the right way to set severance payments is usually done in models with implicit contracting and asymmetric information (see, e.g., Booth and Chatterji 1989, Kuhn 1992, Saha 1993 or Fella 2005). Anyhow, models with implicit contracting hardly address the effects that dismissal protection has on unemployment. Merging the opposed views about the effects of employment protection on unemployment, Levine (1989), Burda (1992), Carter (1992), Saint-Paul (1995), Goerke (2002a), Alvarez and Veracierto (2000) and many others have shown in various model frameworks that the effects of dismissal protection on unemployment highly depend on the design of the employment protection legislation and the wage bargaining structure. The models just mentioned either assume exogenously given wages, efficiency wages or wages individually bargained between workers and firms. In early models with a collective bargaining structure, employment protection has hardly been integrated. Exceptions are the works of Booth (1995b) and Pita (1997), who show that if unions bargain simultaneously over wages and severance payments, the competitive efficient employment level can be achieved. This is because bargaining over severance payments can be considered as a substitute for bargaining over employment itself, and therefore has the effect of the "efficient bargaining model" (see Booth 1995a). Related to such models are the "insider-outsider models" by Lindbeck and Snower (1986, 1987). Sanfey (1995) finds that employment protection has a positive effect on unemployment in such an insider-outsider framework as it increases the insiders' bargaining power.

Nowadays, one of the commonly used model frameworks for the analysis of labour markets and the effects of dismissal regulations is the search and matching approach by Mortensen and Pissarides (1994). This model type itself gives a good microeconomic foundation for unemployment, endogenising employment flows as well as hiring and firing decisions (Manning 1995). Further, it is possible to include different types of wage bargaining structures, namely individual bargaining, the efficiency wage hypothesis, union wage bargaining and insider-outsider bargaining (see Mortensen and Pissarides 1999). First preparations for the current matching models can be found in Phelps (1968), Alchian (1969) or Mortensen (1970). The motivation for this type of model was driven by empirical findings from, e.g., Davis and Haltiwanger (1990, 1992), Blanchard and Diamond (1990) or Blanchflower and Burges (1996), who all find that unemployment and vacancies exist at the same time; a property which is not pictured by most labour market models. The importance of job flow dynamics has also been incorporated into other model types, e.g., by Caballero and Hammour (1994), Bertola and Caballero (1994) or Hopenhayn and Rogerson (1993). Those models describe the job flow dynamics more from a firm's perspective, concentrating on investment decisions, innovation or general equilibrium aspects, while matching models focus on the imperfections of the matching process between workers and firms. Calibration of the Mortensen and Pissarides (1994) model by Cole and Rogerson (1996), e.g., was able to show that, compared the other types of models addressed, matching models seem to capture empirical facts best. Therefore, this model framework has become a standard framework when analysing labour market policies nowadays.

The basic idea of matching models in the manner of Mortensen and Pissarides (1994) is that trade in the labour market is a decentralised and uncoordinated economic activity. If firms decide to create a new job, they have to announce a vacancy, which involves advertisement costs. It takes time before the vacancy is filled, since firms do not find the adequate worker right away. Analogously, workers looking for a job also have to spend some time and effort before they find their "right" employer. The process of firms and workers finding each other is mostly described by a linear homogeneous matching function, positively depending on the number of unemployed workers and vacancies. After a successful match, a job is created and production takes place. Wages are bargained according to a Nash bargaining process in the basic Mortensen and Pissarides (1994) model. The higher the workers' bargaining power, the higher their share of the rents from production is. First extensions with different wage setting structures can be found in Mortensen and Pissarides (1999), as already mentioned above.

Economic shocks can destroy a job. Each job may have a different idiosyncratic productivity. This being the case, economic shocks influence the job-specific productivity. If the productivity falls below some endogenously determined reservation productivity, again, the job is destroyed. Workers' utility maximisation and firms' profit maximisation over time then determine the process of job creation and job destruction and, therefore, employment flows over time. Workers consider that during their life time, there will be phases of employment and unemployment, while firms take into consideration that existing jobs might be destroyed at some moment in time. In equilibrium, or steady state, the changes of endogenously determined variables, such as employment flows, are zero, and therefore an equilibrium unemployment rate can be calculated.

The theoretical analysis of the present work focuses on the effects of employment protection on unemployment. However, it should be noted at this point that for efficiency reasons, some unemployment is not necessarily bad in matching models. This is due to the fact that unemployment eases labour re-allocation and may, therefore, reduce firms' search costs. Hence, there must be a socially efficient rate of job creation and job destruction and, thus, unemployment. The question of efficiency in search equilibrium is already addressed by Phelps (1972) and Tobin (1972), making their efficiency analysis on the basis of the very early models of search economies mentioned above. Relating their results to matching models with two-sided search, equivalent to the model of Mortensen and Pissarides (1994), it has been shown by Hosios (1990) that for a socially efficient outcome, the elasticity of the matching function must equal the bargaining power of workers. This condition has, in principle, been confirmed by many others (see, e.g., Moen 1997, Acemoglu and Shimer 1997 or Pissarides 2000). Hence, in general, the equilibrium resulting in a matching model can be socially inefficient, as there is no theoretical explanation why the barging power of workers should be equal to the elasticity of the matching function.

The effects of policy instruments in matching models has attracted great interest. Employment protection has first been introduced into models of the Mortensen and Pissarides (1994) type by Millard (1995), Lijungqvist (1997) and Mortensen and Pissarides (1999). In their models, dismissal costs have to be paid when the firm decides to lay off a worker. Those dismissal costs are "waste", as they are paid to some third party not endogenised in these models. As layoffs become more expensive, firms decide to dismiss fewer workers. At the same time the additional dismissal cost is anticipated when hiring a worker and decreases the firms' incentive to employ additional workers. Therefore, the effect on unemployment is ambiguous. Garibaldi (1998) chooses another way to model employment protection. In his model, firms cannot dismiss a worker as soon as they have decided to do so. Rather, they have to wait for approval of some authority. This is costly for firms as the layoff is delayed. The resulting effects are similar to the ones described above. Picking up a special form of employment protection, Garibaldi (2004) has shown that notice periods alone have the same ambiguous effects on unemployment as the modelling of general dismissal costs. However, he shows that through increased notice periods, the job-to-job flow increases while the unemployment inflow decreases. With this argument, he is able to explain why unemployment inflows in the United States are smaller than in Europe, but, general job flows are still similar. Related to employment protection is employment subsidisation. Subsidising employment generally increases firms' incentive for job creation and, therefore, reduces unemployment (see, e.g. Holmlund and Linden 1993 or Shi and Wen 1999). While employment subsidies aim at increasing unemployment outflows, employment protection, the subject of theoretical analysis in this work, aims at decreasing unemployment inflows.[2]

The above presented models refer to risk-neutral agents. Neglecting incentive effects for education, innovation, etc. for the moment, risk-neutrality does not really explain why employment protection should exist. Pissarides (2001) presents a matching model with risk-averse workers, while firms are still risk-neutral. The argument for this assumption is that workers have only limited access to credit markets, while firms are able to use these credit markets as some kind of insurance agency. Credit markets are not explicitly modelled though. Pissarides (2001) assumes for simplification that endogenous job destruction does not exist, because risk-aversion and endogenous job destruction yield highly ambiguous effects in the Nash wage bargaining process and the following comparative static analysis. Introducing different labour market institutions, including employment protection, Pissarides (2001) finds that in absence of insurance possibilities for workers, employment protection can compensate for the lack of security. If designed optimally, employment protection does not negatively influence employment and job creation. An optimal design of employment protection includes notice periods and severance payments. Severance payments compensate for the workers' lack of having no access to credit markets. Notice periods make workers search for jobs earlier, because, as they are risk-averse, they try to avoid income losses. Pure administrative dismissal costs are not included in the analysis. Another way to introduce risk-aversion with endogenous job destruction is to assume that wage bargaining does not exist. In this case, workers receive their reservation wage, which is the utility of unemployment

[2]Tilli (2003) finds in a qualitative and quantitative analysis by combining subsidies with unemployment benefits, employment protection and a progressive tax system that hiring subsidies and a progressive taxation not only internalizes search externalities, but can also compensate distortions produced by employment protection and unemployment benefits. His results are based on a simulation with Italian data.

plus the expectation to find a job. This has been done by, e.g., Cahuc and Malherbet (2004).

The literature just discussed concentrates on the effects of employment protection on job creation and job destruction. It seems worth mentioning, though, that Saltari and Tilli (2004) use another approach in a modified Mortensen and Pissarides (1994) framework. They assume a reverse causality between job creation and firing costs and argue that while decentralised job creation causes labour market rigidities, endogenous firing costs then can produce a positive externality. Higher individual job creation increases individual firm's search costs and decreases firing costs. The decrease of firing costs decreases labour turnover costs. Hence, if the decrease of firing costs can offset the increase in search costs, a socially efficient outcome can be achieved.

In Mortensen and Pissarides (1999), different labour market institutions, such as unemployment benefits, different wage bargaining schemes, firing costs and severance payments are integrated. This is important, as we will focus our attention on the effects of employment protection in different institutional settings in the following analysis. In general, severance payments (which are addressed in chapter 5) are qualitatively different to pure firing costs. As they reduce the workers' wage claim, their employment effect is neutral or even positive (see,e.g., Garibaldi and Violante 2002). Similar results have been achieved by Lazear (1990), Fella (2000) or Goerke (2002a) in an efficiency wage framework. However, in these models, it is possible to clearly distinguish whether a worker has been dismissed due to operational reasons or due to disciplinary reasons. Galdón-Sánches and Güell (2003) present an efficiency wage model where this is not the case and dismissal disputes are taken to court. The court might mistakenly allow workers who are not entitled to receive a severance payment to get one and vice versa. They then find that severance payments unambiguously decrease employment, which is the opposite of the findings of Lazaer (1990) and Fella (2000). The reason is that, due to judicial mistakes, firms can no longer anticipate the exact payment they face when dismissing a worker, and therefore reduce employment due to the insecurity. A more detailed overview of the most recent literature addressing severance payments and judicial mistakes can be found in chapter 5, as this is going to be subject of analysis there.

As chapter 4 concentrates on the effects of an experience rated unemployment insurance, we have a brief look at the literature on unemployment benefits and taxation. First approaches introducing unemployment benefits to compensate workers for job destruction being too high can be found in Mortensen (1977). He shows that the existence of unemployment benefits decreases workers' search intensity as the utility of unemployment is increased. This finding has been confirmed by Atkinson and Micklewright (1991). Wang and Williamson (1996), Hopenhayn and Nicolini (1997), Fredriksson and Holmlund (2001) and Albrecht and Vroman (2005) find that the decrease of workers' search intensity can be met by decreasing unemployment benefits over time. Cahuc and Lehman (2000) find the opposite as they stress that declining unemployment benefits over time increase the workers' wage claim which can overcompensate the positive effects of increasing search intensity of unemployed workers.

Taxes increase the workers' gross wage claim and therefore reduce employment (see, e.g., Shi and Wen 1999). However, Pissarides (1998) estimates that a 10% tax cut can reduce unemployment by only one percentage point. Additionally, Hansen (1999) presents a model with a progressive tax system where workers endogenously chose their working time. The more progressive a tax system is, the less attractive it is to work more hours for higher wages. Thus, reducing tax progression increases working hours, wages and unemployment. The questions of taxation and unemployment benefits have been combined by Ljungqvist and Sargent (1995). They assume that workers might quit, looking for better job opportunities. After leaving, they are unemployed until they find another job. Those workers who quit are not entitled to receive unemployment benefits. With a progressive income tax, the distribution of net wages is tightened and, therefore, the incentive for a worker to look for better job alternatives decreases with increasing progression. Hence, a progressive tax system can offset the adverse effects of unemployment benefits on unemployed workers' search intensity as it lowers the number of workers who quit.

A related question to optimal taxation and (unemployment) transfers is to find the optimal way to finance unemployment benefits. First works that have attended this issue are by Feldstein (1976) and Topel and Welch (1980). The question of an optimal system to finance the unemployment insurance has recently attracted some more attention. Lately, Cahuc and Malherbet (2005) and Cahuc and Zylberberg (2005) have addressed this question. They find that an experience rated unemployment insurance unambiguously decreases unemployment. This is due to the fact that the externality arising from financing the unemployment insurance through employment contributions (as already addressed in chapter 1) can be resolved. Further, some authors find that such a financing system can be welfare improving (see, e.g., Fath and Fuest 2005a or Blanchard and Tirole 2005, who use different model frameworks). A more detailed overview about the relevant literature concerning this question is given in chapter 4.

Another institution introduced in matching models is unionisation, which we will refer to in chapter 7. First approaches to introduce unions have been achieved by Mortensen and Pissarides (1999). The basic idea is that the union is organized as a democracy that sets a perfectly egalitarian wage for each member. Outsiders and unemployed workers are excluded from the membership. Insider workers are heterogenous in their idiosyncratic productivity and might have different preferences concerning the wage set by the union. The union therefore chooses the wage for all matches by majority voting. In the case the job value turns negative (due to the chosen wage), firms are free to destroy the job. This set-up corresponds to the classical monopoly union approach, where unions impose their preferred wage level to the firm which then determines employment (see McDonald and Solow, 1981). Garibaldi and Violante (2005) enhanced this setting by allowing for an utilitarian union that takes into account the fact that higher wages impose higher insiders' reservation productivity and, thus, job destruction (which reflects the fact that the union also - at least to a certain extend - considers the level of employment of insiders). Garibaldi and Violante (2005) analyze the effects of severance payments in such a framework. They confirm the famous employment neutrality result of severance payments by Lazear (1990) as long as outsiders remain unconstraint with their individual-level bargaining (because then, the change of severance payments is fully absorbed by a corresponding change in wages). However, they show that when insiders and outsiders are constraint to the wage set by the union, severance payments unambiguously decrease overall employment. Nevertheless, Garibaldi and Violante (2005) assume, following Saint-Paul (2002), that the utility of unemployment is given from the union's point of view. This at least partly drives their results. A more detailed overview of the effects at work is given in chapter 7 as the question of how employment protection affects labour market outcomes in unionised economies is addressed there.

An important issue that has not been addresses in the models presented above are heterogeneous workers which we need to analyse educational effects of employment protection in chapter 6. Generally, the labour force of a country is not homogeneous and workers differ in their ability and their skills. Heterogeneous workers have first been introduced by Kohns (2000) extending the Mortensen and Pissarides (1994) framework with two exogenously given skill groups. He is able to show that high-skilled workers face a lower dismissal probability and shorter unemployment duration. This is empirically confirmed by the OECD (OECD 2004a). In the model by Kohns (2000), worker heterogeneity is introduced by assuming that high-skilled workers generally have a higher productivity than low-skilled workers. This makes high-skilled jobs more productive on average and, therefore, economic shocks hitting low- and high-skilled jobs to the same extend can be better compensated by the high-skilled sector. Thus, the high-skilled sector faces fewer dismissals. Higher productivity and fewer dismissals in the high-skilled sector increase the value of jobs there and yields greater incentives for job creation. This increases re-employment probability in this sector. Wages are generally higher in the high-skilled sector, but do not overcompensate the productivity advantage.

When workers are allowed to choose their education level, Charlot and Decreuse (2005) find that in a matching model with two skill groups, too many workers acquire skills from an efficiency point of view. This is because workers will not take into account their impact of education on other workers' wage and employment perspectives. By introducing firing costs into the model with heterogeneous workers, Kohns (2000) finds that those are more beneficial for employed high-skilled workers than for employed low-skilled workers. This is due to the fact that the additional costs resulting from an increase of employment protection can be better compensated through the higher productivity in the high-skilled sector. However, the incentive for job creation decreases in both sectors, and thus the effect on sector-specific unemployment is still ambiguous. Güelfi (2004) finds similar results. Dolado et al. (2005) therefore suggest to differentiate employment protection across different skill groups in an extended Mortensen and Pissarides (1994) framework. They find through calibrations that those differentiations have different effects on aggregated labour demand than equal employment protection. However, they are not able to clearly identify a politically realisable way of differentiation.

A logical question arising from the fact that highly educated workers have better job market opportunities and benefit more from the same level of employment protection is how employment protection influences education. The main literature incorporating employment protection and education has focused on "on-the-job" training. Bean (1997), Wasmer (2003) and Fella (2005) find that workers' incentive to contribute to the firm increases with higher employment protection due to more job security on the one hand. On the other hand, Burda (2003) has shown that higher employment protection decreases the firms' incentive to invest in the education of their workers as both aspects induce costs. Firms try to compensate additional firing costs by a reduction in education. Similar findings in different model frameworks can be retraced in Südekum and Rühmann (2003). The argument can be made for both firm-specific and general human capital investment (see, e.g.,

Booth and Zoega 2001 or Fella 2000). But to my knowledge, the effects of employment protection on workers' ex-ante skill formation for workers have not been addressed. This question is addressed in chapter 6, where we also find a more detailed overview of the effects of employment protection on "on-the-job" training.

Some more specific literature concerning the questions of the following analysises is addressed in the corresponding chapters. We will also refer to some of the literature mentioned above in more detail.

Chapter 4

Dismissal versus Employment Taxes: Experience Rated Unemployment Insurance

4.1 Introduction

Financing unemployment benefits through employment taxes leads to externalities as firms which are firing workers create additional costs to the unemployment insurance which they do not have to bear. To internalize these externalities, firms can be made liable for their behavior by changing the financing system toward a scheme with dismissal taxes. The proceeds are used to lower employment taxes. Such a financing system can be interpreted as unemployment insurance with experience rating as it exists in the USA (see, e.g., Anderson and Meyer 2000 or Fath and Fuest 2005b). There, employers' contributions to unemployment insurance are differentiated according to the individual employer's dismissal history. For Germany, a proposal for such a change in financing can be found in the 2003 annual report of the German Council of Economic Experts (2003).

Recently, the topic has been addressed by Blanchard and Tirole (2004), Cahuc and Malherbet (2004), and Cahuc and Zylberberg (2005).[1] Blan-

[1]Earlier theoretical contributions are, e.g., Feldstein (1976), Burdett and Wright

chard and Tirole (2004) conclude that dismissal taxes should be part of an optimal design of unemployment insurance to make firms internalize the costs of benefits provided. As they do not use a dynamic model, the effects on the job creation decision of firms are not incorporated. Cahuc and Zylbergerg (2005) present a model of optimal taxation and find that dismissal taxes to finance unemployment insurance could significantly increase employment and GDP. Optimal layoff taxes even exceed expenses of unemployment insurance and include payroll taxes forgone by the state if a worker is dismissed. In their model, they also use an exogenous arrival rate of job offers. The lack of being able to analyze the job creation process has been overcome by Cahuc and Malherbet (2004). They find that while the positive effect on employment remains, job creation decreases when introducing dismissal taxes. The model they use is a matching model with endogenous job creation and destruction. Unemployment insurance is financed by dismissal and employment taxes, while its total expenditure is fixed. On the one hand, the increase of dismissal taxes results in fewer dismissals. On the other hand, job creation is reduced. The first effect dominates the second effect which implies a positive effect on employment.

We present a model where job creation and, therefore, re-employment chances for unemployed workers unambiguously increase when dismissal taxes are raised as long as they do not cover the expected costs for an unemployed worker. At the same time, job destruction is still reduced. Therefore, we find a negative effect on unemployment when increasing dismissal taxes. Our focus is a positive one, explaining the effects that taxes financing unemployment insurance have on job creation and unemployment. Normative aspects will only briefly be referred to in section 4.4.

We use a model which is qualitatively equivalent to that of Cahuc and Malherbet (2004), with two exceptions. These being that the level of unemployment benefits is exogenously fixed while total expenditure is determined endogenously, while Cahuc and Malherbet (2004) regard the level of unemployment benefits as endogenous. As in most countries the level of unemployment benefits per worker is determined by law, which is more or less inflexible in the short and middle term, our modeling seems to be more appropriate.[2] Additionally, we allow for wage bargaining. Cahuc and Malherbet (2004) assume risk-averse individuals but do not allow for wage

(1989), and Marceau (1993).

[2]Note that the chapter does not address the question of which level of unemployment benefits should be paid for efficiency reasons. We take unemployment benefits as given since they exist in nearly every developed country. A theoretical explanation could be to assume that unemployment benefits correspond to the subsistence level. This argumentation is in line with Bovenberg (2003).

bargaining, as workers are assumed to have no bargaining power and, therefore, receive their reservation wage, which equals unemployment benefits. The introduction of wage bargaining forces us to assume risk-neutral agents. But as the special case of workers having no bargaining power is comprised by our assumptions, we can directly relate our results to the findings of Cahuc and Malherbet (2004).

We use a standard matching model with a two-tier wage contract in line with Mortensen and Pissarides (1994, 1999, 2003). Use of dismissal taxes means that the externality that individual employment policies affect other firms is taken into account. When deciding about layoffs, firms and workers only take their individual payoffs into consideration. As a result of the introduction of dismissal taxes, the social costs of layoffs - a rise in unemployment insurance contributions - are internalized. We find that, therefore, employment taxes can be reduced by more than necessary to offset the negative effect of dismissal taxes on the value of the firm. Job creation increases. In Cahuc and Malherbet (2004), who derive a negative effect on job creation, the modeling of the budget constraint yields an additional effect through reservation wages of workers. The increase of dismissal taxes results in fewer dismissals, which decreases unemployment on the one hand. The reduction of unemployment on the other hand increases the wage claim by workers, due to fixed total expenditures of unemployment insurance. This decreases the firms incentive to job creation. As we assume fixed unemployment benefits, the latter effect does not appear in our setting.

One can also relate our results to the discussion about employment protection since experience rating is often considered to be a special form of employment protection (see Mortensen and Pissarides 1999). Interpreting our findings in this manner, we show that employment protection, if designed as experience rating, does not necessarily adversely affect the re-employment possibilities of unemployed workers as it is often claimed (OECD 2004a).[3]

The following analysis is based on Baumann and Stähler (2006)[4] extended by a first pass to a welfare analysis. We will proceed as follows. Section 4.2 describes the basic structure of the model. Section 4.3 deals with the effects of a change in the financing of unemployment insurance.

---

[3]Referring to Belot et al. (2002), the OECD report states that if employment protection gives incentives for workers to invest in firm-specific human capital, "*the resulting productivity gains could compensate for the depressive effect that firing costs may have on job creation*" (OECD 2004a, p. 91). We show that this incentive is not necessary for our results to hold.

[4]To comply with the *Exclusive Licence Agreement* with Labour, we have to note that further information about the article is available at www.blackwell-synergy.com. Parts of it are directly used within this work.

We relate the results to the existing literature and point out the differences of our model. In section 4.4, we provide a first step for analysing first best solutions in the presence of unemployment insurance. In section 4.5, the main findings are summarised.

4.2 The Model

4.2.1 Basic Structure

We consider an economy in continuous time. Population is normalized to one. The labor market is characterized by search frictions. Unemployment u and vacant jobs v exist at the same time. Open positions are filled when an unemployed person matches with a vacancy. This process is described by a linear homogeneous and concave matching function $m(u, v)$. The number of vacancies and therefore market tightness $\theta = v/u$ is determined endogenously and determines the process of job creation. The rate at which vacant jobs are filled is given by $q(\theta) = \frac{m(u,v)}{v} = m(1/\theta, 1)$, where $q'(\theta) < 0$. An unemployed person finds a new job at the rate $\theta q(\theta) = \frac{m(u,v)}{u}$, where $(\theta q(\theta))' > 0$.

Because of the search frictions, economic rents accrue to a matched firm-worker pair. The sharing rule for these rents is determined by Nash-bargaining over wages between firms and workers.

The productivity of existing jobs depends on idiosyncratic productivity shocks. Firm-worker matches will be dissolved when the productivity of the job falls short of some threshold productivity level. This reservation productivity, which governs the process of job destruction, is also determined endogenously.

The government maintains mandatory unemployment insurance. Each unemployed person receives benefits b per period. To finance these benefits, the government can rely on contributions t per employed person (modelled as an employment tax) or dismissal taxes T that have to be paid by firms when laying off a worker.

In what follows, the mathematical structure of the model will be described in more detail in line with Pissarides (2000) and Mortensen and Pissarides (2003).

Each firm has one position to offer which can be either filled (job) or vacant (vacancy). The idiosyncratic productivity of a filled job $\epsilon \in [\epsilon_l, \epsilon_u]$ is distributed according to the cumulative distribution function $G(\epsilon)$, with $g(\epsilon)$ being the corresponding density function. Shocks occur to every single job at the Poisson rate λ. In the case of a shock, a new idiosyncratic productivity is drawn from the distribution $G(\epsilon)$. The value of a firm $J(\epsilon)$ depends on current profits and the option value of a possible shock. Current profits are given by the difference between productivity and gross wages. The latter equals net wages $w(\epsilon)$ and employment tax t. If productivity falls below the endogenous reservation productivity, ϵ_d, the job will be destroyed, in which case the firm has to pay dismissal tax T.

4.2.2 The Value Functions and Wages

Firms

With r being the interest rate in the economy, the Bellman equation for continuing firms reads

$$rJ(\epsilon) = \epsilon - w(\epsilon) - t + \lambda \left[\int_{\epsilon_d}^{\epsilon_u} J(x)dG(x) + G(\epsilon_d)(-T) - J(\epsilon) \right]. \quad (4.1)$$

Newly created jobs are endowed with the highest possible productivity ϵ_u (see Pissarides 2000). Given an initial wage w^0, the Bellman equation for a new job satisfies

$$rJ^0 = \epsilon_u - w^0 - t + \lambda \left[\int_{\epsilon_d}^{\epsilon_u} J(x)dG(x) + G(\epsilon_d)(-T) - J^0 \right]. \quad (4.2)$$

Analogously, we derive the Bellman equation for a vacancy V. Recruitment costs are given by c per period.

$$rV = -c + q(\theta) \left[J^0 - V \right] \quad (4.3)$$

Free entry for firms implies that vacancies will be created as long as their present value is greater than zero. Accordingly, in equilibrium, the condition $V = 0$ has to hold, yielding

$$J^0 = \frac{c}{q(\theta)}. \quad (4.4)$$

Equation (4.4) implies that the present value of a newly created job has to equal the search costs c per period multiplied by the average search duration $1/q(\theta)$.

Workers

Workers are risk-neutral. They can either be employed (with lifetime utility $W(\epsilon)$ in continuing jobs or utility W^0 in a new job) or unemployed (with utility U). If unemployed, they receive unemployment benefits b. Given the probability of finding a new job, the corresponding Bellman equation for the unemployed satisfies

$$rU = b + \theta q(\theta)\left(W^0 - U\right). \tag{4.5}$$

Employed workers earn net wages $w(\epsilon)$ in continuing and w^0 in new jobs. If the productivity of a job falls below the reservation productivity ϵ_d, the worker becomes unemployed. Similar to the description of firms, the Bellman equations depicting the worker's payoffs read

$$rW(\epsilon) = w(\epsilon) + \lambda\left[\int_{\epsilon_d}^{\epsilon_u} W(x)dG(x) + G(\epsilon_d)U - W(\epsilon)\right], \tag{4.6}$$

$$rW^0 = w^0 + \lambda\left[\int_{\epsilon_d}^{\epsilon_u} W(x)dG(x) + G(\epsilon_d)U - W^0\right]. \tag{4.7}$$

Wage Bargaining

Wage bargaining is modelled as a Nash-bargaining procedure between the worker and the firm where β reflects the bargaining power of the worker. Wages are renegotiated in case a shock occurs. In continuing jobs, the fall-back position for the firm is given by the payment T, which has to be made in case of a layoff, while the threat point of workers is given by the utility of an unemployed U. In contrast, if employer and employee bargain over the initial wage before a contract is made, the fall-back position for the employer is given by the value of a vacancy, which equals zero in equilibrium. Therefore, we get a two-tier wage contract supporting

$$w(\epsilon) = \arg\max\left(W(\epsilon) - U\right)^{\beta}\left(J(\epsilon) + T\right)^{1-\beta}, \tag{4.8}$$

$$w^0 = \arg\max\left(W^0 - U\right)^{\beta} J^{0\,1-\beta}. \tag{4.9}$$

The maximisation problems of equations (4.8) and (4.9) imply the sharing rules (for calculations, see Appendix A.1)

$$\beta\left(J(\epsilon) + T\right) = (1-\beta)\left(W(\epsilon) - U\right), \tag{4.10}$$

$$\beta J^0 = (1-\beta)\left(W^0 - U\right). \tag{4.11}$$

The resulting wages are

$$w(\epsilon) = \beta(\epsilon - t + rT + \theta c) + (1-\beta)b, \tag{4.12}$$

$$w^0 = \beta(\epsilon_u - t - \lambda T + \theta c) + (1-\beta)b = w(\epsilon_u) - \beta(r+\lambda)T. \tag{4.13}$$

The two-tier wage structure guarantees that workers share the same rate of dismissal taxes as of employment taxes according to their bargaining power (see Mortensen and Pissarides 2003).

4.2.3 Job Destruction, Job Creation, Unemployment and Equilibrium

For given policy parameters, the market equilibrium is specified by the two endogenous variables market tightness θ and reservation productivity ϵ_d, which govern the processes of job creation and job destruction. The reservation productivity is determined by the job destruction condition that the worker will be dismissed, if the value of the firm falls below the negative dismissal tax, therefore, $J(\epsilon_d) = -T$. As stated earlier, market tightness θ is determined by free market entry for firms, equation (4.4). Following Pissarides (2000), we derive (see Appendix A.2)

$$\epsilon_d - t + \frac{\lambda}{r+\lambda}\int_{\epsilon_d}^{\epsilon_u}(x-\epsilon_d)\,dG(x) = b + \frac{\beta}{1-\beta}c\theta - rT \tag{4.14}$$

as job destruction condition (JD) and

$$\frac{(1-\beta)\,(\epsilon_u - \epsilon_d)}{r+\lambda} - (1-\beta)T = \frac{c}{q(\theta)} \tag{4.15}$$

as job creation condition (JC).

Unemployment is determined by inflows $(\lambda G(\epsilon_d)(1-u))$ and outflows $(\theta q(\theta) u)$ according to the job destruction and job creation decisions of firms. In steady state, the change in unemployment is zero and the unemployment rate is given by

$$u = \frac{\lambda G(\epsilon_d)}{\lambda G(\epsilon_d) + \theta q(\theta)}. \tag{4.16}$$

The state has to finance expenditure on unemployment insurance, bu. The government receives income from employment taxes t per employed person $(1-u)$ and from dismissal taxes T for each worker fired $(\lambda G(\epsilon_d)(1-u))$. Therefore, the government's budget constraint reads

$$bu = t(1-u) + T\lambda G(\epsilon_d)(1-u). \tag{4.17}$$

The equilibrium of the economy is determined by the policy parameters t and T and the corresponding equilibrium values of market tightness θ and reservation productivity ϵ_d (and, of course, the other exogenously given parameters which we consider to be constant in further analysis). The latter two determine the steady state unemployment rate u. The policy parameters are chosen in such a way that the budget for the government is balanced in steady state. Therefore, the corresponding equilibrium values are obtained by simultaneously solving equations (4.14), (4.15), (4.16) and (4.17) for pre-determined t or T.[5]

4.3 Comparative Statics

The following analysis deals with the question of what will happen if the system for financing unemployment benefits is changed to a system where dismissal taxes play a more important role. We restrict our attention to the steady state. Using equations (4.14) and (4.15), we first describe the basic effects of the introduction of dismissal taxes, neglecting the budget constraint, to relate our results to the findings of existing literature on employment protection. In a second step, we investigate the effects of the budget constraint by using equations (4.16) and (4.17) and illuminate the results. We find that under certain conditions, the negative effect of dismissal taxes on job creation is reversed. Therefore, unemployment unambiguously decreases when dismissal taxes are substituted for employment taxes.

Differentiating the JD, equation (4.14), yields

$$-\frac{1}{r+\lambda}\left(r+\lambda G(\epsilon_d)\right)d\epsilon_d+\frac{\beta c}{1-\beta}d\theta=rdT-dt. \tag{4.18}$$

Reservation productivity falls with dismissal taxes T as it becomes more expensive to dismiss an employee. It increases with employment taxes t since, from the point of view of the firm-worker pair, net productivity is decreased.

For the JC, equation (4.15), we obtain

$$-\frac{1-\beta}{r+\lambda}d\epsilon_d-(1-\beta)dT=-\frac{c}{q(\theta)^2}q'(\theta)d\theta. \tag{4.19}$$

Equation (4.19) states that the change in the expected value of a new job equals the change in search costs. The optimal reservation productivity is chosen by the firm according to JD. To get a better understanding of the effects at work, we solve equation (4.18) for the change in reservation

[5] For given dismissal taxes, multiple equilibria may exist. For example, an equilibrium with high employment taxes and high unemployment could exist as well as an equilibrium with low employment taxes and low unemployment. According to Rocheteau (1999a and 1999b), the government can guarantee the lower unemployment rate by setting the policy parameters t and T and adjusting unemployment benefits until the economy reaches the low unemployment equilibrium. As unemployment benefits are considered to be fixed in our setting, the government can only adjust t and T accordingly.

productivity $d\epsilon_d$ and insert the result into the left hand side of equation (4.19). The change in the value of a new job is then given by

$$dJ^0 = -\frac{1-\beta}{r+\lambda G(\epsilon_d)}\left[dt + \lambda G(\epsilon_d)dT\right] - \frac{\beta c}{r+\lambda G(\epsilon_d)}d\theta. \tag{4.20}$$

As the rate at which jobs are destroyed is given by $\lambda G(\epsilon_d)$, the adjusted discount factor for the firm equals $r + \lambda G(\epsilon_d)$. The firm bears part $(1-\beta)$ of an increase in employment taxes t or expected dismissal cost $\lambda G(\epsilon_d)T$ per period. An increase in market tightness θ improves the outside option of workers and thereby wages. The latter fact is described by the last term on the right hand side of equation (4.20).

Neglecting the budget constraint, equations (4.18) and (4.19) can be solved simultaneously to calculate the effects on reservation productivity and market tightness due to changes in the policy parameters t and T (for calculations see Appendix A.3).

$$d\epsilon_d = -\frac{1}{D}\frac{c}{q(\theta)^2}q'(\theta)dt + \frac{1}{D}\left(\frac{rc}{q(\theta)^2}q'(\theta) - \beta c\right)dT \tag{4.21}$$

and

$$d\theta = -\frac{1}{D}\frac{(1-\beta)}{r+\lambda}dt - \frac{1}{D}\frac{(1-\beta)}{r+\lambda}\lambda G(\epsilon_d)dT, \tag{4.22}$$

where

$$D = -\frac{1}{r+\lambda}\left(r+\lambda G(\epsilon_d)\right)\frac{c}{q(\theta)^2}q'(\theta) + \frac{\beta c}{r+\lambda} > 0.$$

An increase in employment taxes t leads to an increase in reservation productivity and a fall in market tightness. Raising employment taxes reduces the net productivity of a given job. This means that the productivity necessary to keep the job active has to increase. At the same time, the value of the firm decreases and therefore fewer vacancies are offered. An increase in dismissal taxes T lowers reservation productivity. Market tightness decreases as well. Raising dismissal taxes directly influence the reservation threshold for an existing job by changing the opportunity outcome for the firm if the employment relationship is dissolved. Therefore, more jobs are held active, but because the value of the firm falls, fewer jobs are created. These findings correspond to the existing literature, pointing out that employment protection will lead to fewer dismissals but at the same time diminish the incentives to creating new jobs.[6] In case of a rise in dismissal taxes, the effect on the unemployment rate is ambiguous because the effects on reservation productivity and market tightness work in opposite directions (see also Mortensen and Pissarides 2003).

Taking into account the budget constraint for unemployment insurance, the ambiguous effect is resolved under certain conditions.

For the budget constraint, equation (4.17), we obtain after totally differentiating

$$dt = \frac{b + t + \lambda G(\epsilon_d)T}{1-u}du - \lambda G(\epsilon_d)dT - \lambda g(\epsilon_d)Td\epsilon_d.$$

Using the budget constraint, equation (4.17), to eliminate t leads to

$$dt = \frac{b}{(1-u)^2}du - \lambda G(\epsilon_d)dT - \lambda g(\epsilon_d)Td\epsilon_d. \tag{4.23}$$

Equation (4.23) states that employment taxes t decrease with decreasing unemployment. With increasing dismissal taxes T, they decrease as a consequence of the direct financing effect of substituting T for t. A decrease in reservation productivity decreases the tax base of dismissal taxes, and therefore employment taxes t have to be increased.

The change of unemployment du is obtained by totally differentiating equation (4.16), which yields

$$du = \frac{\lambda g(\epsilon_d)\theta q(\theta)}{(\lambda G(\epsilon_d) + \theta q(\theta))^2}d\epsilon_d - \frac{\lambda G(\epsilon_d)q(\theta)(1-\eta(\theta))}{(\lambda G(\epsilon_d) + \theta q(\theta))^2}d\theta, \tag{4.24}$$

with $0 < \eta(\theta) = -\frac{\theta q'(\theta)}{q(\theta)} < 1$ being the elasticity of $q(\theta)$. Unemployment decreases with increasing market tightness since more jobs are created and increases with reservation productivity since more jobs are destroyed.

Inserting equation (4.24) into (4.23) yields

$$dt = b\left[\frac{\lambda g(\epsilon_d)}{\theta q(\theta)}d\epsilon_d - \frac{\lambda G(\epsilon_d)q(\theta)(1-\eta(\theta))}{(\theta q(\theta))^2}d\theta\right] - \lambda G(\epsilon_d)dT - \lambda g(\epsilon_d)Td\epsilon_d, \tag{4.25}$$

where the change in unemployment is decomposed into the effects of the changes in market tightness and reservation productivity. There are now

[6] See, for example, Bertola (1990 and 1999), Garibaldi (1998) and Mortensen and Pissarides (2003).

two channels influencing t through reservation productivity ϵ_d. Next to the tax base effect described above, a rise in reservation productivity increases employment taxes t through the unemployment channel. Thereby, as long as dismissal taxes T are smaller than the average costs of an unemployed worker, $\frac{b}{\theta q(\theta)}$, the effect via the unemployment rate dominates the tax base effect.[7]

Solving the system of equations formed by (4.18), (4.19) and (4.25), we derive the effects of a change in dismissal taxes T on reservation productivity and market tightness, taking into account the budget constraint for unemployment insurance. The change in market tightness equals (for calculations see Appendix A.4)

$$d\theta = \frac{1}{Q}(1-\beta)\lambda g(\epsilon_d)\left(\frac{b}{\theta q(\theta)} - T\right) dT, \tag{4.26}$$

where

$$Q = D + \lambda g(\epsilon_d)\left(\frac{b}{\theta q(\theta)} - T\right)\frac{cq'(\theta)}{q(\theta)^2} - b\frac{\lambda G(\epsilon_d)q(\theta)(1-\eta(\theta))}{[\theta q(\theta)]^2}\frac{(1-\beta)}{r+\lambda}.$$

The sign of Q is determined by the combination of the policy parameters t and T. As long as an increase in employment taxes t creates a budget surplus for given dismissal taxes T, the sign of Q is positive (roughly spoken, as long as the equilibrium is on the increasing segment of the Laffer curve - for a proof see Appendix A.5).

Considering equation (4.26), we see that the term in brackets on the right hand side, $\frac{b}{\theta q(\theta)} - T$, is positive as long as average costs of an unemployed worker exceed dismissal taxes. In this case, an increase in dismissal taxes leads to an increase in market tightness for $Q > 0$. Therefore, this kind of employment protection has no adverse effects on job creation. In addition, a simultaneous increase of dismissal taxes and market tightness unambiguously implies a decrease in reservation productivity (see the totally differentiated JC, equation (4.19)).

Summing up, as long as dismissal taxes do not cover the average costs of an unemployed worker and an increase in t leads to a budget surplus ($Q >$

---

[7]Note that $\frac{b}{\theta q(\theta)}$ equals unemployment benefits b multiplied by the mean duration of unemployment $\frac{1}{\theta q(\theta)}$. The unemployment insurance is fully financed by dismissal taxes for $T = \frac{b}{\theta q(\theta)}$, implying $t = 0$. If we did allow for bankruptcy in which case firms are not able to pay dismissal taxes, even when $T = \frac{b}{\theta q(\theta)}$, a positive employment tax, $t > 0$, would be needed for a balanced budget. However, in the presence of bankruptcy, the qualitative results of our analysis do not change.

0), a rise in dismissal tax will increase market tightness, while reservation productivity will decrease. Therefore, unemployment unambiguously falls, in contrast to the results of the effect of pure firing costs (see also equation (4.24)).

This can be explained by the negative externality that results when unemployment benefits are financed by employment taxes t. Dismissals take place if they are efficient from the point of view of the firm-worker pair. Increasing dismissal taxes T makes the two parties take into account the total effect of their decision, and therefore the total burden to finance unemployment insurance given by employment taxes t and dismissal taxes T decreases.[8] The value of new jobs, and therefore market tightness, increases.

As equations (4.20) and (4.25) show, the increase in the value of the firm can be broken down into three effects. An increase of T leads to the direct financing effect of substituting dismissal taxes T for employment taxes t. This nullifies the negative effect of dismissal taxes on the value of the job discussed above. On the one hand, as can be seen in equation (4.25), t and T cannot be fully substituted to achieve the direct financing effect, because fewer dismissals lead to the tax base effect. This makes it necessary to increase employment taxes t to have a balanced budget. On the other hand, as can also be seen in equation (4.25), the decrease in dismissals lowers the financial requirements of unemployment insurance so that t can be decreased. The latter effect dominates the first one as long as dismissal taxes are smaller than the average costs of an unemployed worker. So, in total, firms face less taxes. This results from the internalization of the externalities mentioned. The argument holds as long as an increase in employment taxes t leads to an increase in the revenues of unemployment insurance ($Q > 0$).[9]

An increase of the value of the firm makes more firms enter the market. Market tightness θ increases until it balances the value of newly created firms and search costs. Additionally, this increase also reduces unemployment, and therefore reinforces the decrease in employment taxes.

[8] The two-tier wage contract guarantees that firms and workers share these costs according to their bargaining power even if the proportions of t and T for financing unemployment insurance are changed.

[9] If the system were located on the downward sloping part of the Laffer-curve ($Q < 0$), the changes in t mentioned above would be reversed and market tightness would decrease. The effect on unemployment would then be ambiguous.

4.4 A First Pass to a First Best in the Presence of Unemployment Benefits

In the model we use, with risk-neutral and infinitively lived agents, efficiency of equilibrium can be characterised by the present value of production (see Pissarides 2000, p. 188). Analogously to the derivation of the Hosios condition (Hosios 1990), we show that in our setting, where the government guarantees a minimum income for unemployed workers, a first-best equilibrium is reached for specific values of the bargaining power of workers β and dismissal taxes T. First, we characterise the first-best by maximising the present value of production by directly controlling for market tightness and reservation productivity, following Pissarides (2000, pp.188 ff). Second, we compare the resulting conditions with the job creation and job destruction conditions resulting in a market equilibrium and determine optimal values for β and T.

4.4.1 Determining the First-Best

The present value of production Ω is determined by

$$\Omega = \int_0^\infty e^{-r\tau}[y - c\theta u]d\tau, \tag{4.27}$$

where y equals the current production and $c\theta u = cv$ constitute search costs. τ represents time. Unemployment benefits are not taken into account separately as they are financed out of current production. The evolution of current production y is given by

$$\dot{y} = \frac{dy}{d\tau} = \theta q(\theta)u\epsilon_u + \lambda(1-u)\int_{\epsilon_d}^{\epsilon_u} \epsilon dG(\epsilon) - \lambda y, \tag{4.28}$$

and the change of the unemployment rate equals

$$\dot{u} = \frac{dy}{d\tau} = \lambda G(\epsilon_d)(1-u) - \theta q(\theta)u. \tag{4.29}$$

By maximising equation (4.27) subject to (4.28) and (4.29) we can describe the socially optimal values of reservation productivity ϵ_d and market tightness θ by the two equations[10]

$$\epsilon_d - \frac{\eta(\theta)}{1-\eta(\theta)}c\theta + \frac{\lambda}{r+\lambda}\int_{\epsilon_d}^{\epsilon_u}(z-\epsilon_d)dG(z) = 0, \tag{4.30}$$

[10] The calculation is perfectly equivalent to Pissarides (2000, p. 189) and is therefore not repeated here.

and

$$(1-\eta(\theta))\frac{\epsilon_u-\epsilon_d}{r+\lambda}=\frac{c}{q(\theta)}. \tag{4.31}$$

These two equations jointly determine the optimal values of θ and ϵ_d, maximising the value of total production minus search costs.

4.4.2 Market Equilibrium

Market equilibrium is characterized by equations (4.14) to (4.17), that is the job destruction and job creation conditions, the unemployment rate and the budget constraint. Inserting equation (4.16) into (4.17), we calculate the employment tax in equilibrium as

$$t=b\frac{\lambda G(\epsilon_d)}{\theta q(\theta)}-\lambda G(\epsilon_d)T \tag{4.32}$$

Using equation (4.32), the equilibrium values of market tightness and reservation productivity are described by the reformulated job destruction condition, equation (4.14),

$$\epsilon_d-b\left(1+\frac{\lambda G(\epsilon_d)}{\theta q(\theta)}\right)-\frac{\beta}{1-\beta}c\theta+\frac{\lambda}{r+\lambda}\int_{\epsilon_d}^{\epsilon_u}(x-\epsilon_d)dG(x)+(r+\lambda G(\epsilon_d))T=0, \tag{4.33}$$

and the job creation condition, equation (4.15),

$$(1-\beta)\frac{\epsilon_u-\epsilon_d}{r+\lambda}-(1-\beta)T=\frac{c}{q(\theta)}, \tag{4.34}$$

restated here for convenience.

4.4.3 Comparison of the Market Equilibrium and the First-Best Solution

For the market to reach a first-best allocation, market tightness θ and reservation productivity ϵ_d have to equal the corresponding values resulting from equations (4.30) and (4.31). Therefore, subtracting equation (4.33) from (4.30) and (4.34) from (4.31), the resulting equations have to equal zero for the market equilibrium to be efficient. The resulting equations are

$$\left(\frac{\beta}{1-\beta}-\frac{\eta(\theta)}{1-\eta(\theta)}\right)c\theta+b\left(1+\frac{\lambda G(\epsilon_d)}{\theta q(\theta)}\right)-(r+\lambda G(\epsilon_d))T=0 \tag{4.35}$$

and

$$(\beta - \eta(\theta))\frac{\epsilon_u - \epsilon_d}{r + \lambda} + (1 - \beta)T = 0. \tag{4.36}$$

Combining equations (4.35) and (4.36) to eliminate dismissal taxes T finally yields

$$\begin{aligned}
&(\beta - \eta(\theta))\frac{r + \lambda G(\epsilon_d)}{r + \lambda}(\epsilon_u - \epsilon_d) \\
&+(1 - \beta)\left(\frac{\beta}{1 - \beta} - \frac{\eta(\theta)}{1 - \eta(\theta)}\right)c\theta \\
&+(1 - \beta)b\left(1 + \frac{\lambda G(\epsilon_d)}{\theta q(\theta)}\right) = 0.
\end{aligned} \tag{4.37}$$

For positive unemployment benefits b, the last term on the left-hand-side of equation (4.37) is positive and the equation can only be fulfilled for $\beta < \eta(\theta)$, that is, workers' bargaining power being lower than the elasticity of the matching function with respect to unemployment.[11] Substituting this result, $\beta < \eta(\theta)$, into equation (4.36), for the market equilibrium to be efficient, dismissal taxes have to be positive as the first term in equation (4.36) is negative.[12]

4.5 Conclusion

The main conclusions of this chapter can be summarized as follows. A rise in dismissal taxes increases market tightness, when the budget constraint for unemployment insurance is taken into account. Reservation productivity falls. Therefore, the unemployment rate unambiguously decreases. This holds as long as dismissal taxes do not cover the average costs of an unemployed worker and an increase in employment taxes leads to a surplus of the budget for unemployment insurance for a given level of dismissal taxes.

Neglecting the budget constraint, the model describes the standard effects that occur in matching models after the introduction of dismissal taxes. On the one hand, reservation productivity decreases, which leads to fewer dismissals. But, on the other hand, market tightness decreases as well, which leads to the creation of fewer vacancies. The effect on the unemployment rate is ambiguous.

[11]For $b = 0$ the Hosios condition (Hosios 1990) applies, $\beta = \eta(\theta)$.

[12]For $b = 0$ and therefore $\beta = \eta(\theta)$ optimal dismissal taxes amount to zero, $T = 0$.

Introducing the budget constraint for unemployment insurance yields an increase in market tightness because the externalities arising from the use of employment taxes to finance unemployment insurance are resolved by the introduction of dismissal taxes. The financial requirements of unemployment insurance decrease due to fewer dismissals. This effect dominates the tax base effect resulting from lower proceeds for the unemployment insurance of dismissal taxes. Therefore, employment taxes can be reduced by more than the equivalent increase in dismissal taxes. The tax burden of firms to finance unemployment insurance decreases, which augments the value of new jobs and makes it more attractive for firms to supply vacancies.

The results are less clear cut if the assumption that a two-tier wage contract exists is weakened to the extent that workers directly renegotiate wages. In this case, the influence of dismissal taxes on unemployment highly depends on the bargaining power of workers. As workers cannot be forced to accept a lower wage at the beginning of the employment relationship, firms have to bear dismissal taxes in full, while employment taxes are effectively shared between firms and workers. If workers have no bargaining power, the above presented results still hold. But if workers have positive bargaining power, the positive effect on market tightness is reduced and may even be reversed.

The analysis presented above does not primarily address the question of welfare effects. It mainly focuses on the effects dismissal taxes have on unemployment. However, in matching models, unemployment does not necessarily decrease welfare, as it eases labor reallocation. Pissarides (2000, chapter 8), in accordance to the well-known Hosios condition (Hosios 1990), illustrates that if the bargaining power of workers is equal to the elasticity of the matching function with respect to unemployment, the welfare-maximising output and unemployment rate result. This result holds in a setting without an endogenously financed unemployment insurance. In our model, the government guarantees a minimum income for each worker through unemployment benefits. In addition, these benefits are financed by employment and dismissal taxes. It can be shown that, to reach a first-best allocation, the worker's bargaining power must be lower than the elasticity of the matching function with respect to unemployment while a positive level of dismissal taxes is needed. A lower bargaining power of workers than implied by the Hosios condition (Hosios 1990) is required because unemployment benefits strengthen the bargaining position of workers by increasing their alternative income. This results in higher wages which lead to a higher reservation productivity and lower market tightness. These effects can partly be balanced by decreasing the bargaining power of workers.

Furthermore, dismissal taxes have to be positive as the distortion of the decision to dismiss a worker due to unemployment benefits is not balanced by the lower bargaining power of workers alone. Nevertheless, a thorough normative analysis concentrating on the welfare effects of experience rating in matching models should be the subject of further research.

Chapter 5

Firing Costs, Severance Payments, Judicial Mistakes and Unemployment

5.1 Introduction

In the discussion about employment protection, it is often claimed that severance payments have some desirable advantages compared to pure firing costs. Firing costs are usually modelled to be "waste that disappears" when a dismissal takes place, while severance payments are paid to the worker in case he is laid off. This yields an advantage of severance payments over pure firing costs, i.e. that workers accept lower wages and, therefore, the firms' incentive of job creation increases (see Lazear 1990). This has been confirmed by, e.g., Fella (2000), Goerke (2002a), and Garibaldi and Violante (2005). In political discourse, especially in continental Europe, the demand for a system of severance payments is steadily rising. For example, in Germany, the German Council of Economic Experts has repeatedly proposed a switch from a system of pure firing restrictions to a system of severance payments in their reports of the year 2005 and 2006 (German Councli of Economic Experts 2005, 2006). The models mentioned above highlighting the superiority of severance payments over pure firing costs consider full information where only those workers that are entitled actually receive the payment.

In most countries, only operational dismissals involve severance payments, while no severance payments have to be paid due to disciplinary or personal dismissals (OECD 2004a). This evokes the incentive for firms to claim the dismissal to be a disciplinary or personal one, while workers claim it to be an operational one. The employee is mostly entitled to insist on a judicial review of the dismissal (OECD 2004a). That gives room to the assumption that judges or juries possibly make mistakes in such a review. The judicial review of the dismissal can create two types of mistakes. First, mistakenly allowing someone who is not entitled to a severance payments (in the following, a shirker) to receive one, type I. Second, not allowing someone who is entitled to a severance payment (in the following, a non-shirker) to receive one, type II. The existence of those mistakes might change the results about the positive employment effect of severance payments.

In theoretical literature, the implications of judicial mistakes have hardly been discussed. One of the first and only papers to analyze the implications of the existence of judicial mistakes on employment is by Galdón-Sánches and Güell (2003). They present a modified efficiency wage model in the manner of Shapiro and Stiglitz (1984) with severance payments. They claim that in the presence of judicial mistakes, "*disciplinary dismissals will not be costless and firing costs will have a negative effect on aggregated employment*" (Galdón-Sánches and Güell 2003, p. 323). This is mainly due to the fact that the severance payment cannot be fully neutralized through an accordant decrease of wages as in complete and perfect markets by anticipating these payments as it is in Lazear (1990). In their model, Galdón-Sánches and Güell (2003) take operational dismissals as an exogenous event, which highly drives their results. They do not compare severance payments to pure firing costs.

In the present chapter, we will do two things. First, we introduce the firm's decision of when to dismiss a worker. The effect of increasing the level of severance payments on unemployment will be by far less clear cut in the presence of judicial mistakes as is claimed by Galdón-Sánches and Güell (2003). The main reason for the difference is that workers will have to be compensated for a higher risk of dismissal through higher wages when firms decide to dismiss earlier. Second, we compare pure firing costs with severance payments.

The problem is analyzed in a matching model according to Mortensen and Pissarides (1994) to be able to explicitly model operational dismissals and the decision of job creation endogenously. To introduce true disciplinary dismissals, the matching model is augmented by the possibility of shirking in the manner of Shapiro and Stiglitz (1984). We show theoretically that a reduction of type I and type II mistakes decreases unemployment. This is due to the fact that decreasing insecurity of dismissal costs lowers expected labour costs and, therefore, unemployment. Furthermore, we see that an increase of the level of severance payments itself has ambiguous effects on job creation and job destruction and, therefore, on unemployment. It does not necessarily increase unemployment as claimed by Galdón-Sánches and Güell (2003). While we are able to derive clear theoretical conditions for unemployment to decrease we cannot say if they are fulfilled. This shows that it is essential to do more empirical research to clarify these conditions and to be able to give political advice and evaluate political actions.

The rest of the chapter is organized as follows. In section 5.2, we will introduce the model. Section 5.3 contains a comparative static analysis. Last, section 5.4 concludes.

5.2 The Model

5.2.1 Basic Structure

We consider an economy with a continuum of infinitely lived, homogeneous workers. The continuum is normalized to one. Firms are also measured in a continuum, while free market entry determines their number. Agents discount at rate r. Workers' instantaneous utility function is given by $V(w, e) = w - e$, where w is the wage income and e characterizes the cost of effort when working.

Following Mortensen and Pissarides (1999), all firms are identical and have one vacancy to offer. The labour market is characterized by search frictions. Unemployment u and vacancies v exist at the same time. The production flow of a firm-worker match is described by a value function and shall in the following be called job. The matching process is described by a linear homogeneous and concave matching function $m(v, u)$. The ratio $\theta = v/u$ is called market tightness. It is determined endogenously. The rate at which vacancies are filled is given by $q(\theta) = m(1/\theta, 1)$, where $q'(\theta) < 0$. Unemployed workers find a job at rate $\theta q(\theta) = m(\theta, 1)$, where $[\theta q(\theta)]' > 0$. Furthermore, each job has an idiosyncratic productivity component $\epsilon \in [\epsilon_l, \epsilon_u]$, which is distributed according to the cumulative and continuously differentiable distribution function $G(\epsilon)$, with $g(\epsilon) > 0$ being the corresponding density function. Productivity shocks occur to every single job at the Poisson rate λ. In the case of a shock, a new idiosyncratic productivity is drawn from the distribution $G(\epsilon)$. If the productivity falls below some endogenously determined threshold value (which is called reservation productivity), the job is destroyed.

We assume that according to Shapiro and Stiglitz (1984), firms need the worker to work at an effort level $e = \bar{e}$ to be productive. That is, when employed, the worker decides if he provides the effort level or not. Effort is a binary choice. Workers can either work (at the effort $e = \bar{e}$) or shirk (where the effort level is $e = 0$). Inspections occur according to a Poisson process with an exogenous arrival rate q and are costless. If a worker is found shirking, at $e = 0$, he is dismissed.

Workers are entitled to receive a severance payment S when they are dismissed due to operational reasons. If dismissed due to disciplinary reasons (shirking), workers miss out. This gives the incentive for firms to claim the dismissal has taken place due to shirking, even though it has been due to a productivity shock. Workers have the incentive to claim that the dismissal has taken place due to operational reasons even though it was due to disciplinary ones. This conflict is taken to court.[1] When laying off a worker, firms have to pay a severance payment S to the worker in the case of an operational dismissal and firing costs T to some third party not explicitly modeled. Judges might make mistakes in the reviewing process. Therefore, following Güell (1999), with exogenous probability m, true disciplinary dismissals are mistakenly judged to be operational layoffs. With probability $(1 - z)$, redundancies are mistakenly judged to be disciplinary dismissals.

5.2.2 The Value Functions and Wages

Workers

The value function for an employed worker, denoted by W, who maximises his life-time utility, satisfies the following Bellman equation

$$rW = \max_{e=0 \text{ or } e=\bar{e}} \{w - e + ql(e)\left[U + mS - W\right] \\ + \lambda \left[\int_{\epsilon_d}^{\epsilon_u} W dG(\epsilon) + G(\epsilon_d)(U + zS) - W \right] \Big\}, \tag{5.1}$$

[1]Note that in the below described model, all disputes are settled in court, because no costs occur from taking the dispute there. Since we are interested in the isolated effects of judicial mistakes, this simplifying assumption does not harm the following analysis. For a first, simple approach of introducing costs associated with going to court, see Galdón-Sánches and Güell (2003). Even there, everybody goes to court as long as the expected benefit from going to court is higher than the punishment when caught lying.

where w is the wage the worker earns. $l(e)$ is a function of the effort e which equals one in the case of $e = 0$ and is zero in the case of $e = \bar{e}$. Therefore, the "asset pricing" function for an employed worker is influenced by the wage minus the effort plus the option value in the case of a productivity shock and the option value in the case a shirking worker is dismissed. If productivity falls below the reservation productivity ϵ_d, the match is resolved and the worker becomes unemployed. In this case, the worker obtains the utility of an unemployed worker U and a redundancy payment S with probability z. If the productivity after the shock does not fall below the reservation productivity, the employment relationship continues, which is expressed in the integral over ϵ_d to ϵ_u, as a new productivity is drawn from the distribution function $G(\epsilon)$. In case the worker is fired due to disciplinary reasons, the worker also receives the utility of unemployment and the redundancy payment S with probability m.

The "asset pricing" function of unemployment can be stated as

$$rU = \theta q(\theta)\,[W - U]\,. \tag{5.2}$$

For simplicity we abstract from non-labour income. Therefore, the utility flow of unemployment equals the option value of finding a job.

To prevent shirking, the worker must get a high enough rent from working for shirking not to pay, i.e. $\underset{e=\bar{e}}{W} \geq \underset{e=0}{W}$. This gives the non-shirking-condition (NSC),

$$W - U \geq \frac{\bar{e}}{q} + mS. \tag{5.3}$$

Equation (5.3) states that a shirker saves the work disutility $\bar{e}$, but bears a capital loss $W - U$ if he is fired after being caught shirking. This event occurs at Poisson rate q. When being fired, a shirker additionally receives a redundancy pay S with probability m.

Using equation (5.1) in combination with equation (5.3), the latter can be transformed to

$$w^e \geq rU + \bar{e} + (r + \lambda G(\epsilon_d))\left[\frac{\bar{e}}{q} + mS\right] - \lambda G(\epsilon_d)zS,$$

where w^e is the non-shirking wage. $rU + \bar{e}$ represents the opportunity cost from working, $(r + \lambda G(\epsilon_d))\left[\frac{\bar{e}}{q} + mS\right]$ the annuity of the rent and $\lambda G(\epsilon_d)zS$ the "belated" wage payment in form of severance payments according Lazear (1990). Using equations (5.2) and (5.3) to eliminate U, we obtain

$$w^e = \bar{e} + [r + \theta q(\theta) + \lambda G(\epsilon_d))]\left[\frac{\bar{e}}{q} + mS\right] - \lambda G(\epsilon_d)zS. \tag{5.4}$$

As long as the NSC is fulfilled, no worker shirks in equilibrium. If it is not, all workers shirk. A high effort level, represented by $\bar{e}$, and high re-employment probability, represented by $\theta q(\theta)$, clearly increase the non-shirking wage, as they increase the opportunity costs of working. Further, higher type I mistakes, rising m, increase the non-shirking wage. This is because, through high type I mistakes, shirkers can falsely receive severance payments in the case of being caught shirking, which increases the incentive to shirk. Lower type II mistakes, rising z, decrease the non-shirking wage, as the expected compensation for a job loss is high, which makes shirking less attractive. Due to the fact that effort of workers is not perfectly observable and judicial mistakes exist, severance payments might reduce workers' incentive to provide effort, which has empirically been confirmed by Riphahn (2004). Intuitively, a high dismissal probability, represented by $\lambda G(\epsilon_d)$, increases the non-shirking wage, as workers have to be compensated for the higher risk of a job loss. Fella (2000) and Baumann (2006) already pointed out that for no judicial mistakes ($m = 0$ and $z = 1$), and for $S = \frac{\bar{e}}{q}$ ($S > \frac{\bar{e}}{q}$), the worker gets fully (over)compensated for the risk of losing the job. Because the severance payment in the above model framework is assumed to be legally determined as in Staffolani (2002), we assume without loss of generality that there is no overprotection and that, therefore, $(z - m)S < \frac{\bar{e}}{q}$ holds. Thus, an increase in reservation productivity and, therefore, dismissal probability, augments the non-shirking wage. A high level of severance payments should decrease the non-shirking wage, as workers get compensated for their job loss by the "belated wage payment" (see again, e.g., Fella 2000). In the presence of judicial mistakes, this effect is ambiguous, as the incentive for shirking also increases with higher severance payments. A high enough type II mistake, low z, can lead to an increase of the non-shirking wage when severance payments are increased. For a given ϵ_d, this is the case if $\frac{m}{z} > \frac{\lambda G(\epsilon_d)}{r+\lambda G(\epsilon_d)+\theta q(\theta)}$ (see equation (5.4)).[2]

Firms

Analogously to the argumentation of the workers' optimization problem, the firm's Bellman equation can be written as

$$rJ(\epsilon) = \bar{e}\epsilon - w^e + \lambda \left[\int_{\epsilon_d}^{\epsilon_u} J(x)dG(x) - G(\epsilon_d)(zS + T) - J(\epsilon) \right]. \quad (5.5)$$

[2]Note that for the case of no judicial mistakes, $m = 0$ and $z = 1$, the non-shirking wage decreases with increasing severance payments through the "belated wage payment" as in Lazear (1990) or Fella (2000). Through judicial mistakes, this is weakened and might be reversed.

The firm's "asset pricing" function therefore consists of the effort level needed, $\bar{e}$, multiplied with the idiosyncratic productivity minus the non-shirking wage plus the option value of a shock. In the case that productivity falls short of the reservation productivity ϵ_d, the firm has to pay firing costs T and a severance payment S with probability z. As the firm knows that it has to pay at least the non-shirking wage (equation (5.4)) to prevent workers from shirking for all wages w below the non-shirking wage, the job would be closed.

The Bellman equation for a vacancy V can be derived in the same manner. Following Pissarides (2000), newly created jobs are endowed with the highest possible productivity, ϵ_u. Recruitment costs are given by $c > 0$ per period.

$$rV = -c + q(\theta)\left[J(\epsilon_u) - V\right]. \tag{5.6}$$

Free market entry for firms implies that vacancies will be created as long as their present value is greater than zero. Accordingly, in equilibrium, $V = 0$ has to hold, yielding

$$J(\epsilon_u) = \frac{c}{q(\theta)}. \tag{5.7}$$

Equation (5.7) states that the value of a newly created job has to equal average search costs.

5.2.3 Job Destruction, Job Creation, Unemployment and Equilibrium

For given policy parameters and judicial mistakes, the market equilibrium is defined by the two endogenous variables market tightness, θ, and reservation productivity, ϵ_d, governing the processes of job creation and job destruction. As long as the expected value of a job exceeds the expected dismissal costs, the job will stay on the market. Therefore, reservation productivity is determined by

$$J(\epsilon_d) = -(zS + T).$$

As stated earlier, market tightness θ is determined by free market entry for firms, equation (5.7). Substituting the wage equation (5.4) into equation (5.5) and using the above described job destruction condition, as well as equation (5.7), we derive (for calculations see Appendix A.6)

$$\bar{e}\epsilon_d + \frac{\lambda \bar{e}}{r+\lambda}\int_{\epsilon_d}^{\epsilon_u} (\epsilon - \epsilon_d)\, dG(\epsilon) + \lambda G(\epsilon_d) zS =$$

$$\bar{e} + [r + \lambda G(\epsilon_d) + \theta q(\theta)] \left[\frac{\bar{e}}{q} + mS\right] - r(zS + T) \tag{5.8}$$

as the job destruction condition (further JD) and

$$\frac{\bar{e}[\epsilon_u - \epsilon_d]}{(r+\lambda)} - (zS + T) = \frac{c}{q(\theta)} \tag{5.9}$$

as the job creation condition (further JC).

Equations (5.8) and (5.9) simultaneously determine the equilibrium values of reservation productivity ϵ_d and market tightness θ for given policy parameters S and T and the judicial mistakes m and $(1 - z)$.

Note that the possibility of multiple equilibria exists. While the JC has a negative slope in the $\epsilon_d - \theta -$space, the JD does not necessarily have a positive slope. It might partly be negatively sloped or S-shaped as presented in figure 5.1. This is due to the positive feedback between the efficiency wage, w^e, and the reservation productivity. An increase of the reservation productivity, ϵ_d, increases the left hand side and the right hand side of the JD, equation (5.8). Because the wage also increases with market tightness, θ, (see equation (5.4)) it can be shown that a necessary and sufficient condition for the JD to have a negative slope is

$$\lambda g(\epsilon_d) \left[\frac{\bar{e}}{q} + (m - z)S\right] > \frac{\bar{e}}{r+\lambda} [r + \lambda G(\epsilon_d)],$$

which means that the marginal effect of an increase of reservation productivity on wages exceeds the marginal increase of the production value of a job at reservation productivity, the left hand side of equation (5.8).[3]

Unemployment is determined by inflows $(\lambda G(\epsilon_d)(1 - u))$ and outflows $(\theta q(\theta) u)$ according to the job destruction and job creation decisions of firms. The equilibrium unemployment is, therefore, also determined by the equilibrium values of reservation productivity and market tightness. In steady state, the change in unemployment is zero and the unemployment rate is given by

$$u = \frac{\lambda G(\epsilon_d)}{\lambda G(\epsilon_d) + \theta q(\theta)}. \tag{5.10}$$

[3]For the discussion about stability, see section 5.3 and Mortensen and Pissarides (1999).

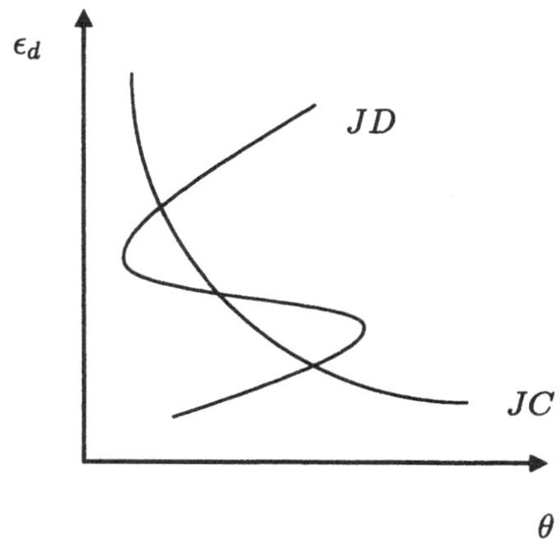

Figure 5.1: Possible Multiple Equilibria with a Non-Shirking Wage

Since, as already mentioned above, no worker shirks in equilibrium, because firms pay the non-shirking wage, no inflows into unemployment result from real disciplinary dismissals in equilibrium.

5.3 Comparative Statics

In the following section, we will analyze the effects of a change of the level of pure firing costs, type I mistakes, type II mistakes, and the level of severance payments. The effects are summarised in Table 5.1. Further, we discuss the results and compare the effects of severance payments to those of firing costs. Calculations can be retraced in Appendix A.7.

5.3.1 Increasing Firing Costs

By totally differentiating the JD and the JC, we find that an increase of the level of firing costs yields

$$\frac{d\epsilon_d}{dT} = \frac{1}{D}\left\{-r\frac{c}{q(\theta)^2}q'(\theta) + [\theta q(\theta)]'\left[\frac{\bar{e}}{q} + mS\right]\right\}, \tag{5.11}$$

and

$$\frac{d\theta}{dT} = \frac{1}{D}\left\{\frac{\bar{e}}{r+\lambda}\lambda G(\epsilon_d) - \lambda g(\epsilon_d)\left[\frac{\bar{e}}{q} + (m-z)S\right]\right\}, \tag{5.12}$$

where

$$D = \left[\frac{\bar{e}}{r+\lambda}(r+\lambda G(\epsilon_d)) - \lambda g(\epsilon_d)\left[\frac{\bar{e}}{q} + (m-z)S\right]\right]\frac{c}{q(\theta)^2}q'(\theta)$$
$$-\frac{\bar{e}}{r+\lambda}\left[\frac{\bar{e}}{q} + mS\right][\theta q(\theta)]'. \tag{5.13}$$

The sign of equation (5.13) is ambiguous. D represents the determinant of the Jakobi matrix of the system of equations (5.8) and (5.9) for the changes of reservation productivity ϵ_d and market tightness θ. If the equilibrium is located on the upward sloping part of the JD, $D < 0$, as

$$\left[\frac{\bar{e}}{r+\lambda}(r+\lambda G(\epsilon_d)) - \lambda g(\epsilon_d)\left[\frac{\bar{e}}{q} + (m-z)S\right]\right] > 0.$$

Therefore, this equilibrium is locally stable. Only if the equilibrium is located on the downward sloping part of the JD, $D > 0$ is possible. In this case, the above equation is negative. However, the equilibrium is locally stable as well, because

$$\left[\frac{\bar{e}}{r+\lambda}(r+\lambda G(\epsilon_d)) - \lambda g(\epsilon_d)\left[\frac{\bar{e}}{q} + (m-z)S\right]\right] + \frac{c}{q(\theta)^2}q'(\theta) < 0.$$

Nevertheless, we know from empirical literature that an increase of firing costs decreases dismissal probability (reservation productivity) and job creation (market tightness).[4] Also, most theoretical works, as, e.g., Bertola (1990), Garibaldi (1998), Mortensen and Pissarides (1999) or Pissarides (2001) approve this result. In the above model framework, this can only be the case if the equilibrium is located on the upward sloping part of the JD, because only there both terms in brackets of equations (5.11) and (5.12) are positive, while $D < 0$. In accordance with empirical and theoretical findings we therefore assume that this relationship holds in the present model as well and $D < 0$ shall be assumed henceforth.

Equations (5.11) and (5.12) then show that reservation productivity and market tightness unambiguously decrease when firing costs are increased, while the effect on unemployment is ambiguous due to fewer dismissals and less job creation, as can be seen in equation (5.10). As dismissals get more expensive, it is clear that reservation productivity and, therefore, dismissal probability decreases. It is also straightforward to argue that through higher firing costs, the value of newly created jobs decreases, and, therefore, in equilibrium, market tightness decreases.

[4] A variety of empirical papers confirms this result, see Addison and Teixeira (2003), Baker et al. (2005) Blanchard and Portugal (2001) and Scarpetta (1996), just to mention a few. Also, it has again been approved by the OECD (OECD 2004a).

5.3.2 Increasing Type I Mistakes

For an increase of type I mistakes, we find again, after totally differentiating the JD and JC, that

$$\frac{d\epsilon_d}{dm} = \frac{1}{D}\left\{\frac{c}{q(\theta)^2}q'(\theta)\left[(r+\lambda G(\epsilon_d)+\theta q(\theta)\right]S\right\} > 0, \tag{5.14}$$

and

$$\frac{d\theta}{dm} = \frac{1}{D}\left\{\frac{\bar{e}}{r+\lambda}\left[(r+\lambda G(\epsilon_d)+\theta q(\theta)\right]S\right\} < 0, \tag{5.15}$$

for $D < 0$. Equation (5.14) shows that reservation productivity increases with increasing judicial mistakes of falsely allowing a shirker redundancy payments. Market tightness decreases when doing so (see equation (5.15)).

The reason for this is straightforward. As can be seen in equation (5.4), a greater judicial mistake rate m increases the non-shirking wage, which is the minimum wage that firms have to pay. Higher wages yield higher labour costs. Therefore, reservation productivity increases. The increase of reservation productivity additionally increases the non-shirking wage. As working costs increase, relatively less jobs are more productive. The value of newly created jobs decreases and, therefore, fewer vacancies are offered.

Thus, increasing the judicial mistakes of falsely allowing a shirker to receive severance payments increases reservation productivity and decreases market tightness. This makes unemployment unambiguously rise if type I mistakes increase, as can be seen in equation (5.10).

5.3.3 Increasing Type II Mistakes

For the change of the type II mistakes of falsely not allowing a non-shirker to receive a severance payment, we find after totally differentiating the JD and JC for $D < 0$ that

$$\frac{d\epsilon_d}{dz} = \frac{1}{D}\left\{-\frac{c}{q(\theta)^2}q'(\theta)(r+\lambda G(\epsilon_d)) + \left[\frac{\bar{e}}{q}+mS\right]\left[\theta q(\theta)\right]'\right\}S < 0, \tag{5.16}$$

and

$$\frac{d\theta}{dz} = \frac{1}{D}\left\{-\lambda g(\epsilon_d)\left[\frac{\bar{e}}{q}+(m-z)S\right]\right\}S > 0. \tag{5.17}$$

Note that to be consistent with the above part, when analyzing the effect of an increase of type I mistakes, we will also analyze an increase of type II mistakes here. But because the type II mistake rate is defined as $(1-z)$, an increase of type II mistakes implies $dz < 0$.

Equation (5.16) shows that reservation productivity increases with increasing judicial mistake of falsely not allowing a non-shirker for redundancy pays. Market tightness decreases when doing so (see equation (5.17)).

This can be explained as follows. First, an increase in the judicial mistakes $(1-z)$ increases the non-shirking wage, because workers have to be compensated for the loss of security of receiving a severance payment when being dismissed as a non-shirker (see equation (5.4)). Labour costs increase. Second, the expected costs of dismissals (zS) decrease, which makes the firm decide to lay off workers earlier according to the JD (see equation (5.8)). Therefore, reservation productivity increases. Through higher wage costs, the value of newly created firms decreases. Even though the expected firing costs zS (and, thus, expected labour costs) decrease, this is overcompensated by the wage increase. That is due to the fact that regarding wages, the decrease of expected severance payments cannot overcompensate the increase of reservation productivity which includes the extra risk compensation. Thus, in total, the value of a newly created job decreases, which decreases the offer of vacancies and, therefore, market tightness (see equation (5.17)).

Hence, increasing the judicial mistakes $(1-z)$ increases reservation productivity and market tightness. This yields more dismissals, and at the same time, less job creation. Therefore, higher type II mistakes yield a higher unemployment rate (see equation (5.10)).

5.3.4 Increasing the Level of Severance Payments

A change of the level of severance payments yields

$$\begin{aligned}\frac{d\epsilon_d}{dS} &= \frac{1}{D}\left\{\left(\frac{c}{q(\theta)^2}q'(\theta)\left((r+\lambda G(\epsilon_d)+\theta q(\theta))m-(r+\lambda G(\epsilon_d))z\right)\right)\right.\\ &\quad\left.+[\theta q(\theta)]'\left[\frac{\bar{e}}{q}+mS\right]z\right\}, \qquad (5.18)\end{aligned}$$

and

$$\frac{d\theta}{dS}=\frac{1}{D}\left\{\left(\frac{\bar{e}}{r+\lambda}(r+\lambda G(\epsilon_d)+\theta q(\theta))\right)m-\lambda g(\epsilon_d)\left[\frac{\bar{e}}{q}+(m-z)S\right]z\right\}. \qquad (5.19)$$

Equations (5.18) and (5.19) show that the effects of an increase of the level of severance payments on reservation productivity and market tightness are ambiguous. They crucially depend on the magnitude of both types of judicial mistakes.

Through an increase of the level of severance payments, expected dismissal costs zS unambiguously increase which gives incentive for firms to decrease reservation productivity, as dismissals get more expensive. Additionally, increasing the level of severance payments has an effect on the non-shirking wage. This effect is ambiguous due to the existence of judicial mistakes (see equation (5.4)). We know from equation (5.18) that reservation productivity increases (yielding more dismissals) due to an increase of the level of severance payments if

$$\frac{m}{z} > \frac{r + \lambda G(\epsilon_d)}{r + \lambda G(\epsilon_d) + \theta q(\theta)} - \frac{1}{(r + \lambda G(\epsilon_d) + \theta q(\theta))\frac{cq'(\theta)}{q(\theta)^2}} \frac{dw^e}{d\theta}, \qquad (5.20)$$

where $\frac{dw^e}{d\theta} = [\theta q(\theta)]' \left[\frac{\bar{e}}{q} + mS\right] > 0$. From equation (5.19), we find that market tightness unambiguously decreases if

$$\frac{m}{z} > \frac{\lambda g(\epsilon_d)\left[\frac{\bar{e}}{q} + (m - z)S\right]}{\frac{\bar{e}}{r+\lambda}(r + \lambda G(\epsilon_d) + \theta q(\theta))} < 1. \qquad (5.21)$$

The combination of equations (5.20) and (5.21) shows that if equation (5.20) holds, equation (5.21) must hold as well as the right hand side of equation (5.20) exceeds the one of equation (5.21).[5] The reasoning for reservation productivity to increase and market tightness to decrease as long as equations (5.20) and (5.21) hold is as follows: Equation (5.20) states that reservation productivity increases with the level of severance payments if the relation of the probability of having to pay a severance payment to a shirker and the probability of having to pay a severance payment to a non-shirker is in a way such that the increase of (direct) labour costs is not compensated by the decrease of (indirect) costs resulting from the anticipated decrease of market tightness. Otherwise, reservation productivity will decrease. This gets obvious when decomposing equation (5.20) into its three components.

First, from differentiating equation (5.4) with respect to S, we know that an increase of the level of severance payments increases the non-shirking

[5] Because for $D < 0$, $\left[\frac{\bar{e}}{r+\lambda}(r + \lambda G(\epsilon_d)) - \lambda g(\epsilon_d)\left[\frac{\bar{e}}{q} + (m - z)S\right]\right] > 0$ holds. Further, the right hand side of equation (5.21) must be smaller than one due to the same argument, $\left[\frac{\bar{e}}{r+\lambda}(r + \lambda G(\epsilon_d)) - \lambda g(\epsilon_d)\left[\frac{\bar{e}}{q} + (m - z)S\right]\right] > 0$.

wage, if $\frac{m}{z} > \frac{\lambda G(\epsilon_d)}{r+\lambda G(\epsilon_d)+\theta q(\theta)}$, i.e., because the type I mistake rate is relatively large, the potential rise of the incentive not to shirk due to the "belated wage payment" cannot compensate the increase of the incentive to shirk due to the fact that shirkers falsely receive severance payments. This augments wage costs and makes firms want to raise reservation productivity on the one hand.

Second, on the other hand, higher severance payments increase dismissal costs and, therefore, make the firm want to decrease reservation productivity, expressed by the term $\frac{r}{r+\lambda G(\epsilon_d)+\theta q(\theta)}$ (see equation (5.8)). This second effect could theoretically compensate for the first effect which means that the type I mistake rate must increase relatively to a type II mistake rate (expressed by the relation $\frac{m}{z}$) for reservation productivity to still be increased by the firm.

Third, the simultaneous increase of reservation productivity and the level of severance payments reduces market tightness as the value of newly created jobs decreases. In equilibrium, this is anticipated by the firm when deciding about the change of reservation productivity. Decreasing market tightness decreases the non-shirking wage ($\frac{dw^e}{d\theta} > 0$) and search costs ($-\frac{c}{q(\theta)^2}q'(\theta) > 0$). This reduces labour costs and gives incentive to decrease reservation productivity. Again, if the relation of type I mistake to type II mistake is big enough (equation (5.20) holds), this effect is compensated by the direct wage increase resulting from an increase of the level of severance payments.

Summing up, we can say that as long as equation (5.20) holds and, therefore, equation (5.21) holds as well, an increase of the level of severance payments raises reservation productivity and decreases market tightness. Therefore, unemployment unambiguously increases (see equation (5.10)).

If equation (5.20) does not hold, but equation (5.21) does, reservation productivity and market tightness decrease. In this case, the direct increase of labour costs resulting from an increase of reservation productivity is overcompensated by the indirect decrease resulting from the anticipation of the decrease in market tightness. This reduces reservation productivity. But the fall of reservation productivity, which increases the value of newly created jobs, cannot compensate the direct negative effect of a decrease of the value of newly created jobs resulting from the increase of the level of severance payments (see equation (5.21)). Therefore, market tightness still falls. The effect on unemployment is ambiguous due to fewer dismissals and less job creation.

If neither equation (5.20) nor equation (5.21) hold, reservation productivity decreases and market tightness increases when increasing the level of severance payments. Hence, unemployment decreases.

5.3.5 Summary and Discussion

From a theoretical point of view, the effects of pure firing costs on reservation productivity and market tightness are not clear cut in a model framework with the possibility of shirking and endogenous dismissal decision as presented above, because there is a positive feedback between the non-shirking wage and reservation productivity (see also Mortensen and Pissarides 1999). Still, it seems reasonable to assume that pure firing costs decrease the dismissal probability and job creation (which yields ambiguous effects on unemployment). This is confirmed by a huge amount of theoretical and empirical studies, as shown in section 5.3.1. Nevertheless, it has to be mentioned that assuming this coherence in the model presented above (and, therefore, $D < 0$) highly drives the results. If we actually found ourselves in the implausible situation where the equilibrium is located on the downward sloping part of the JD and $D > 0$, the above results would change signs.

A very clear point of the above analysis is that judicial mistakes, both type I and type II, increase unemployment. This becomes easily obvious in sections 5.3.2 and 5.3.3. Therefore, it seems desirable to keep those mistakes small if one is interested in a low unemployment rate. The model does not analyse where those mistakes come from and takes them as exogenously given. It simply highlights the implications the existence of those mistakes has. If we accept that such mistakes exist, we then see that they have negative effects on employment. This chapter clearly gives the assignment to empirical researchers to estimate the magnitudes of those mistakes to see if the topic does have relevance. For theoretical researchers, the assignment is to investigate the origin of those mistakes and to examine a cost/benefit analysis to see if the costs to reduce these mistakes can be compensated by the benefits of a low unemployment rate. So far, there is no empirical literature estimating the magnitude of judicial mistakes. But the existing literature hints that those mistakes do exist. Bertola et al. (1999) find that in Spain and France about one employee in 200 appealed to the courts in 1995. In those countries, over 70% of the cases were won by workers. For Germany, in 2001, 27% of all dismissal disputes were taken to court (German Council of Economic Experts 2003). Also, Goerke and Pannenberg (2004) find in a more detailed analysis that between 1990 and 2002 in Germany, on average, 14% of all employment relationships terminated were accompanied by severance payments. Additionally, Ichino et al. (2003) find that in Italy, 22% of all dismissals are taken to court and after all, 17% of the dismissals are overruled by court. Furthermore, they show in an empirical and (game) theoretical approach that judges might be biased by the labour market situation when settling the dismissal dispute. They find out that a bad labour market situation can influence judges' decision in favour of the worker.[6] Also, Berger (1998) finds that court rules have been significantly more in favour of workers in phases of downswings in Western Germany. This at least allows for the assumption that a judicial review needs some interpretation and errors might occur (either by mistake or even deliberately). For a good overview of existing regulations concerning employment protection laws and severance payments, see Bertola et al. (1999), OECD (2004a) or chapter 2. Bertola et al. (1999), too, hint at the fact that judicial mistakes most probably exist, but also say that it is very hard to gather decent data about this issue.

What is not so clear is the effect of an increase of the level of severance payments on unemployment. As section 5.3.4 shows, the effect can be ambiguous due to fewer dismissals and less job creation, or positive due to more dismissals and less job creation, or negative due to fewer dismissals and more job creation. This depends on the relation of the type I and type II mistake rates. Table 5.1 summarizes the effects from the above presented theoretical analysis, where (+) indicates a positive, (−) a negative and (?) an ambiguous effect.

Change of	**Reaction of**		
	$d\epsilon_d$	$d\theta$	du
$dm > 0$	(+)	(−)	(+)
$dz < 0$	(+)	(−)	(+)
$dT > 0$	(−)	(−)	(?)
$dS > 0$	(?)	(?)	(?)

Table 5.1: Effects of dm, dz, dT, and dS

Despite the ambiguity of the effects of an increase of the level of severance payments, we are able to keep hold of the following. If there were no judicial mistakes or if they are relatively small ($m \approx 0$ and $z \approx 1$), an increase of the level of severance payments decreases unemployment as has been shown in section 5.3.4. Therefore, in this case, severance payments effectively dominate pure firing costs in fighting unemployment as claimed by the authors mentioned in section 5.1. The opposite holds for very large judicial mistakes ($m \approx 1$ and $z \approx 0$). In all the cases in between those

[6] Ichino et al. (2003) use firm level data of one specific firm which they do not name. Therefore, the empirical results might not reflect the situation in Italy.

extremes, the analysis of section 5.3.4 applies.

Putting those results into the perspective of existing literature, we can now say that the result by Galdón-Sánches and Güell (2003), namely that an increase of the level of severance payments unambiguously increases unemployment, only holds for large judicial mistakes or relatively large type I mistakes in relation to relatively small type II mistakes. Their result only represents one possible outcome and is very much driven by the assumption that no endogenous dismissal probability and, therefore, no feedback between the firms' layoff decision and wages exists. Relaxing this assumption leads to the results presented in section 5.3.4. Further, Galdón-Sánches and Güell (2003) assume that $m = z$ and show that it does not make any difference in their analysis if $m \neq z$. In the above model, it makes a difference. Following Galdón-Sánches and Güell (2003), and assuming that $m = z$, we can see that market tightness unambiguously decreases. This can easily be confirmed by equation (5.21), where the right hand side is smaller than unity and $\frac{m}{z} = 1$ for $m = z$. From equation (5.20), we find for $m = z$ that if the indirect cost decrease of wage and search costs is smaller than unity ($1 > -\frac{1}{cq'(\theta)/q(\theta)^2}\frac{dw^e}{d\theta}$), reservation productivity increases and the results of Galdón-Sánches and Güell (2003) apply. Otherwise, it decreases, which yields ambiguous effects on unemployment due to an increase of the level of severance payments.

5.4 Conclusion

This chapter contributes to the discussion about severance payments and firing costs if workers' effort is not perfectly observable and judicial mistakes exist when deciding who is entitled to receive a severance payment and who is not. In contrast to Galdón-Sánches and Güell (2003), we allow for endogenous job destruction and job creation, permitting firms to decide when to dismiss a worker. It is shown that when the effects of pure firing costs on unemployment are ambiguous due to fewer dismissals and less job creation, the existence of type I and type II mistakes unambiguously increase unemployment. This is mainly due to the fact that the existence of those mistakes increases the incentive of shirking (because through a type I mistake, a shirker might receive the severance payment when dismissed and through a type II mistake, a non-shirker might not receive the severance payment). This increases wages and, therefore, labour costs yielding more dismissals and less job creation. In contrast to the model by Galdón-Sánches and Güell (2003), an increase of the level of severance payments generates ambiguous effects on job destruction and job creation and, therefore, unemployment. We are able to derive conditions for unemployment to increase or decrease, depending on the magnitude of type I and type II mistakes. For relatively small (or no) judicial mistakes, an increase of the level of severance payments decreases dismissals and increases job creation. Hence, an increase of the level of severance payments can increase employment.

This chapter points out that is is essential to learn more about judicial mistakes when dealing with employment protection in form of severance payments. It gives clear assignments for further research. As the existence of judicial mistakes clearly has negative effects on employment (with and without a change of the level of severance payments), further theoretical research should detect the origin of judicial mistakes as they are taken as exogenously given in the present chapter. Additionally, one should find incentives to decrease judicial mistakes. Empirical research should try to clarify the magnitude of judicial mistakes to examine the relevance of dealing with them. As already mentioned, this has not really been tackled. There are hints that such mistakes exist though. If one finds out that they are large and, therefore, of importance, political advice concerning severance payments might have to be changed.

Chapter 6

Employment Protection and Ex-Ante Incentives for Skill Formation

6.1 Introduction

By comparing the data on the population percentage with tertiary education in each country with country-specific indices of the level of employment protection, as found in the the recent OECD reports (OECD 2004a and 2004b), we see that countries with high levels of employment protection tend to have a higher percentage of population with tertiary education. This observation seems to hold particularly in the European context. In countries rated as having relatively high employment protection, such as Belgium, Finland, Germany, the Netherlands, and Norway, the percentage of the population with tertiary education exceeds the average level within all OECD countries.

Furthermore, in the OECD employment report (OECD 2004a) it is empirically shown that shorter unemployment duration, better re-employment probabilities and fewer dismissals are an accompaniment of education. But it is claimed in the report itself that "*still, little is known about the labour market impact of (...) learning.*" (OECD 2004a, p. 183).

Next to the fact that the present chapter gives a theoretical explanation for shorter unemployment duration, better re-employment chances and fewer dismissals of highly educated workers, it especially focuses on the effect that employment protection has on the ex-ante decision of individuals to obtain education. The existing literature that incorporates employment protection with education solely concentrates on education obtained "on-the-job" (see below a brief description of the literature in more detail). However, a huge part of individual skill formation takes place before entering the labour market (for example, the decision whether to get a university degree or not) as the OECD report (2004b) shows.

Effects of employment protection on education have been analysed in models where education is considered to be "on-the-job training". Fella (2005) shows in a model with incomplete contracting that termination restrictions increase the firm's and the worker's incentive to invest in training. In his model, termination restrictions do not only include employment protection for workers, but he also investigates penalties in cases where the worker leaves. The reason for more training is that the restrictions assure a higher probability of obtaining benefits from the training investment for both sides, the firm and the worker. Burda (2003) presents a matching model with endogenous education decision. He models education as human capital investment made by firms. He finds through calibration that more employment protection decreases the incentive for education. While employment protection and "on-the-job training" both induce some costs for the firm, stronger employment protection results in lower education because the firm attempts to compensate for the additional costs of more employment protection by reducing education. In addition, Wasmer (2003) points out that the education decision is not independent of the aggregated state of the labour market. In particular, he shows that through different employment protection rules in the US and Europe, different investments in (specific and general) human capital can partly be explained. The investment in general and human capital is obtained by the worker "on-the-job". If employment protection is low, workers invest less in specific and more in general human capital as their general human capital will be rewarded in the case of a job loss. For sufficiently high employment protection, though, their expected returns of specific human capital investments will compensate for the risk of loosing the job (which is now lower with stronger employment protection) and, therefore, induces them to invest more in specific human capital. The argument is in agreement with Bean (1997), who claims that more job security may increase the worker's contribution to the firm. An ex-ante decision on skill formation of workers has been introduced by Sato and Sugiura (2003). They analyse the effects of subsidies on human capital investments and unemployment benefits on skill formation.

In the present chapter, firstly, we contribute to the discussion of the effects of employment protection on general human capital investment. We assume that only workers will decide whether they get educated or not. Secondly, we make an additional remark on the discussion that skill formation does not (only) take place "on-the-job" but is done ex-ante by the workers themselves (see OECD 2004b). As employment protection affects "on-the-job" skill formation, it is reasonable to ask the question which effect employment protection has on the ex-ante education decision of workers. Using a matching model in line with Mortensen and Pissarides (1994, 1999, 2003) with two skill groups, we show that, in contrast to Burda (2003), more employment protection increases the incentive to skill formation as long as the worker obtains a sufficiently large fraction of this investment and the education decision is taken by the worker ex-ante.

The following chapter is based on Stähler (2006). We will proceed as follows. Section 6.2 describes the basic model. Section 6.3 deals with the effect of a change in employment protection on the labour market, education and unemployment. Section 6.3.2 calibrates the basic model to provide some additional insight. Stähler (2006) is extended in sections 6.4 and 6.5, where dismissal costs are allowed to differ in each sector (section 6.4) and where workers receive severance payments (section 6.5). In section 6.6, the main findings are summarised.

6.2 The Model

6.2.1 Basic Structure

The economy is populated by a continuum of individuals which is normalised to one. The economy is continuous in time, and individuals die at rate δ. They are replaced by new born individuals without education at the same rate. At the beginning of their lives and, therefore, before they enter the labour market, each individual has to decide whether to become educated or not. Firms are also measured in a continuum, while their number is determined by the condition of free market entry.

Firms supply jobs, and workers offer their work. The productivity of jobs determines how many jobs are supplied and whether existing jobs are destroyed. These two features are captured in the job creation and the job destruction conditions. Unemployment exists due to market frictions and matching problems between employers and employees. There are two separate labour markets, one for the low-skilled and one for the high-skilled. Once educated, high-skilled workers do not move into the low-skilled sector.

The number of high-skilled workers shall be denoted by $A^s = \tilde{x}$ and the number of low-skilled workers by $A^l = (1 - \tilde{x})$, respectively. A Cobb-Douglas matching function, equal in both sectors, $M(A^i u^i, A^i v^i)$, with the typical properties and $i = l, s$ for low- and high-skilled is assumed to capture the market frictions and indicate that job-seeking takes time.[1] The sector-specific unemployment rate is denoted by u^i, while v^i is the corresponding vacancy rate. Unemployment and vacancies exist at the same time. We define the ratio $\theta^i = A^i v^i / A^i u^i = v^i / u^i$, which is called market tightness.

Note that it could be reasonable to assume that the matching processes in the high- and low-skilled sector differ. The qualitative results of the following analysis are not influenced by such an assumption. Therefore, for simplicity, we do without the differentiation and assume the matching function to be equal in both sectors.[2]

The rate at which vacancies are filled is the number of matches, given by the matching function, divided by the number of vacancies in the corresponding sector. In terms of the market tightness, this can be written as $q(\theta^i)$, with $q'(\theta^i) < 0$. Analogously, the probability of an unemployed worker finding a job in each sector can be calculated as $\theta^i q(\theta^i)$ with $(\theta^i q(\theta^i))' > 0$.

The productivity of a given job can be decomposed additively into a global component $p + a^i$, with $a^s > 0$ and $a^l = 0$, and an idiosyncratic component ϵ^i. The idiosyncratic component is a zero-mean shock with $\epsilon^i \in [\epsilon_l; \epsilon_u]$. ϵ^i is distributed according to the cumulative distribution function $G(\epsilon^i)$, with $g(\epsilon^i)$ being the corresponding density function and being equal in both sectors. Shocks occur to every job at a Poisson rate λ. The shock changes the idiosyncratic productivity, drawing a new ϵ^i out of the distribution. If the idiosyncratic productivity falls below the endogenous reservation productivity ϵ_d^i, the job will be destroyed.

There are vacancy costs c for each vacancy. Employment protection is represented by dismissal costs T which have to be paid by the firm when firing a worker. T is equal in both sectors since we assume the same level of employment protection to hold for each skill group. T can be interpreted as legal costs for dismissals.

---

[1] Petrongolo and Pissarides (2001, pp. 396) claim that *"(t)he stylized fact that emerges from empirical literature is that there is a stable aggregate matching function of a few variables that satisfies the Cobb-Douglas restrictions with constant returns to scale in vacancies and unemployment"*. Therefore, the loss of generality assuming a Cobb-Douglas matching function can be justified by the consistence of such a function with empirical facts. Furthermore, it simplifies the analysis later on.

[2] For a Cobb-Douglas matching function, the differentiation can simply be done by assuming functions of the form $M^s(A^s u^s, A^s v^s) = (A^s u^s)^{\alpha}(A^s v^s)^{(1-\alpha)}$ and $M^l(A^l u^l, A^l v^l) = (A^l u^l)^{\sigma\alpha}(A^l v^l)^{(1-\sigma\alpha)}$, where $0 < \alpha, \sigma\alpha < 1$, for example. We will briefly refer to the resulting quantitative difference in section 6.3.

Employers and employees bargain over wages according to a Nash-bargaining process. The wages depend on the job-specific productivity. It is assumed that after each shock the wages are renegotiated. Following Pissarides (2000), only unemployed workers look for a job, while the employed stay on their job until they are dismissed or die.

We assume that individuals are low-skilled at the beginning of their lives, but heterogeneous in their ability to learn. Ability (necessary learning effort, respectively) x is uniformly distributed in an interval $x \in [0, 1]$, with zero representing the highest ability (i.e. lowest learning costs). The lower an individual's ability to learn, the more units of education x an individual needs to become high-skilled. A unit of education costs k. Education takes place infinitely fast at the beginning of the period when the individual is born.

To decide whether to get educated or not, each individual compares the utility value of being low-skilled with the utility value of being high-skilled minus the individual costs of education. We assume that in case of equality, the individual gets educated. As we assume a uniform skill distribution and because the population size is normalized to unity, the resulting threshold value of x is equal to $\tilde{x}$. Each individual with $x > \tilde{x}$ will stay low-skilled (and vice versa). The game structure is arranged according to the following time line.

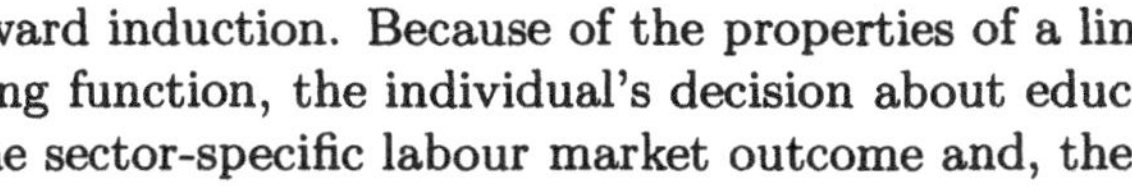

In the first step, after individuals have been born, they make their education decision and then, in the second step, enter the labour market. The labour market outcome is then determined as described above. The game is solved by backward induction. Because of the properties of a linear homogeneous matching function, the individual's decision about education does not influence the sector-specific labour market outcome and, therefore, the education decision of others. This is fairly important, and we will return to this point in more detail later on, when turning to the education decision. In the following analysis, we are going to describe the structure of the labour market and then explain the education decision.

6.2.2 The Value Functions and Wages

Firms

In both sectors, each firm has one job to offer which can be either filled or vacant. The number of firms is endogenously determined. The value of the firm $J(\epsilon^i)$ depends on the productivity (overall and idiosyncratic), wages $w(\epsilon^i)$ and the option value. Therefore, the value of the firm satisfies the Bellman equation

$$(r+\delta)J(\epsilon^i) = p+a^i+\epsilon^i-w(\epsilon^i)+\lambda\left[\int_{\epsilon_d^i}^{\epsilon_u} J(x)dG(x) + G(\epsilon_d^i)(-T) - J(\epsilon^i)\right]. \tag{6.1}$$

r is the interest rate of the economy. In the case of a dismissal, which occurs with probability $\lambda G(\epsilon_d^i)$, firms have to pay the amount T to some third party.

Following Pissarides (2000), newly created jobs are endowed with the highest possible idiosyncratic productivity and satisfy the Bellman equation

$$(r+\delta)J^{0,i} = p+a^i+\epsilon_u^i-w^{0,i}+\lambda\left[\int_{\epsilon_d^i}^{\epsilon_u} J(x)dG(x) + G(\epsilon_d^i)(-T) - J^{0,i}\right], \tag{6.2}$$

with $w^{0,i}$ as initial wage payment.

Analogously to the above formula, we can derive the Bellman equation for a vacancy V^i as

$$rV^i = -c + q(\theta^i)\left[J^{0,i} - V^i\right]. \tag{6.3}$$

The possibility of free market entry for firms implies that vacancies will be created as long as their present value is greater than zero. Accordingly, in equilibrium, $V^i = 0$ holds. Therefore equation (6.3) implies

$$J^{0,i} = \frac{c}{q(\theta^i)} \tag{6.4}$$

in equilibrium. Equation (6.4) says that the discounted value of a newly created job has to equal the search costs c per period multiplied with the average search duration $1/q(\theta^i)$.

Workers

Workers can either be employed (with utility $W(\epsilon^i)$) or unemployed (with utility U^i). If they are unemployed, they get the option value of finding a job, since, we assume for simplicity that there are no unemployment benefits. The Bellman equation for the unemployed satisfies

$$(r+\delta)U^i = \theta^i q(\theta^i)\left(W^{0,i} - U^i\right), \tag{6.5}$$

where $W^{0,i}$ is the utility of a newly founded job. The equation for an employed worker reads

$$(r+\delta)W(\epsilon^i) = w(\epsilon^i) + \lambda \left[\int_{\epsilon_d^i}^{\epsilon_u} W(x)dG(x) + G(\epsilon_d^i)U^i - W(\epsilon^i) \right]. \quad (6.6)$$

The employed workers obtain the utility of the wage (depending on the sector the corresponding worker is working in) and the option value of a change in the idiosyncratic component. If the idiosyncratic component falls below a certain value ϵ_d^i, the job is destroyed and the corresponding worker becomes unemployed. If the job has just been created, the corresponding Bellman equation for a newly employed worker is given by

$$(r+\delta)W^{0,i} = w^{0,i} + \lambda \left[\int_{\epsilon_d^i}^{\epsilon_u} W(x)dG(x) + G(\epsilon_d^i)U - W^{0,i} \right]. \quad (6.7)$$

Wage Bargaining

Wage bargaining is modelled as a Nash bargaining procedure between workers and firms, where the bargaining power of workers is β. The workers' fall back utility is the utility of unemployment, U^i, while the firms' fall back utility are the negative dismissal costs, $-T$. The bargaining can be represented as $w(\epsilon^i) = argmax \left(W(\epsilon) - U^i\right)^\beta \left(J(\epsilon) + T\right)^{1-\beta}$ for the wage of continuing jobs and $w^{0,i} = arg\, max \left(W^0 - U^i\right)^\beta J^{0,i\,1-\beta}$ for newly created jobs, because when firms and workers bargain for the first time, firms do not face the threat of having to pay the dismissal costs in the case bargaining fails (see Mortensen and Pissarides 2003). The resulting wages are $w(\epsilon^i) = \beta[p + a^i + \epsilon^i + (r+\delta)T + c\theta^i]$ and $w^{0,i} = w(\epsilon_u) - \beta(r+\delta+\lambda)T$.[3]

6.2.3 Job Destruction, Job Creation, Education, Unemployment and Equilibrium

Job Destruction and Job Creation

Using these wages, we can derive the Job Destruction Condition (further JD), which describes under which circumstances a job is destroyed, as

$$p + a^i + \epsilon_d^i + \frac{\lambda}{r+\lambda+\delta} \int_{\epsilon_d^i}^{\epsilon_u} \left(z - \epsilon_d^i\right) dG(z) = \frac{\beta}{1-\beta} c\theta^i - (r+\delta)T, \quad (6.8)$$

[3]The wage bargaining is in perfect analogy to chapter 4. Therefore, see also Appendix A.1 for calculations with $b = t = 0$ and $\delta > 0$.

and the Job Creation Condition (further JC), which shows when jobs are created and therefore determines market tightness θ^i. It can be derived from using equation (6.4) and equalises the cost of searching with the productive value of a job for the employer. Hence, it can be stated as[4]

$$\frac{(1-\beta)\left(\epsilon_u - \epsilon_d^i\right)}{r+\lambda+\delta} - (1-\beta)T = \frac{c}{q(\theta^i)}. \tag{6.9}$$

By solving equations (6.8) and (6.9) simultaneously, one obtains the reservation productivity ϵ_d^i and the market tightness θ^i in each sector. Because of the higher sector-specific productivity $p + a^s$ in the high-skilled sector, there is a lower job destruction rate in the high-skilled sector than in the low-skilled sector. Jobs remain productive longer and are, therefore, destroyed later than in the low-skilled sector. This yields $\epsilon_d^s < \epsilon_d^l$ and $\theta^s > \theta^l$. Empirical research tends to confirm this hypothesis, as can be seen in Boeri et al. (2004).

The Education Decision

Individuals enter the labour market unemployed. The utility value of an individual is therefore represented by equation (6.5).[5] Thus, for an individual to get educated, the utility of being unemployed for the high-skilled worker minus the individual costs of education has to equal or exceed the utility of being unemployed of the low-skilled worker, $U^s - kx \geq U^l$. The threshold value of x for an individual to still be willing to get educated can thereby be calculated as $\tilde{x} = \frac{U^s - U^l}{k}$.

In equilibrium, $W^{0,i} - U^i = \frac{\beta c}{(1-\beta)q(\theta^i)}$ holds (see Appendix A.1 or Pissarides 2000, p. 41, where $V^i = 0$ in steady state and, therefore, $J^{0,i} = \frac{c}{q(\theta^i)}$). Substituting this into (6.5) leads to $U^i = \frac{\beta c}{(1-\beta)(r+\delta)}\theta^i$ which yields

$$\tilde{x} = \frac{\beta c}{(1-\beta)(r+\delta)k}(\theta^s - \theta^l). \tag{6.10}$$

As equation (6.10) shows, there is no education without bargaining power ($\beta = 0$). This is because without bargaining power, workers only receive their reservation wage. This is true across both sectors. The higher the bargaining power, the higher the worker's share of a firm-worker-pair. Therefore, the worker receives higher payoffs on his education investment.

[4] Calculations are in analogy to chapter 4 and can be retraced in Appendix A.2 for $b = t = 0$ and $\delta > 0$.

[5] For this kind of modeling see also Kolm and Larsen (2003), Sato and Sugiura (2003) or Pissarides (2000, chapter 7).

Equation (6.10), furthermore, states that the decision to get educated mainly depends on the differences between the market tightnesses and, therefore, on the probabilities of finding a job in each sector. The market tightness in each sector is determined in the second stage of the game, which is the labour market outcome. This outcome influences the education decision of individuals before they enter the labour market. But the education decision itself does not influence the labour market outcome in the second stage.

This is due to the matching function, which is linear homogeneous, and the free market entry for firms. Independent of how many people in the economy are low- or high-skilled, in a steady state, the sector specific market tightness remains the same for given exogenous parameters.[6] Therefore, the individual's decision which sector to go to does not affect the decision of others and vice versa. The outcome of the second stage of the game (the labour market outcome) enters into the first stage (education decision) as a given parameter, while the first stage does not influence the second stage of the game. If more people decide to become educated, more vacancies in the high-skilled sector are supplied. Therefore, the original sequential structure can be dropped, as there is no reaction function of individuals.

Unemployment

Unemployment is determined by inflows $(\lambda G(\epsilon_d^i)(1-u^i)A^i + \delta A^i)$ into and outflows $(\theta^i q(\theta^i)u^i + u^i A^i \delta)$ out of unemployment in each sector. In steady state the changes of unemployment will be zero. Thus, the steady state unemployment rate for each sector can be derived as

$$u^i = \frac{\lambda G(\epsilon_d^i) + \delta}{\lambda G(\epsilon_d^i) + \theta^i q(\theta^i) + \delta}. \tag{6.11}$$

To calculate the total number of unemployed in the whole economy, we multiply the unemployment rate (6.11) with the corresponding number of workers in this sector A^i and add the resulting numbers of unemployed workers of each sector ($u^* = u^l(1-\tilde{x}) + u^s\tilde{x}$). Since population is normalised to one, u^* simultaneously gives the total number of the unemployed in the

[6] In the end, market tightness in each sector only depends on unemployment and vacancy rates, not on the number of people in each sector. Increasing the number of, for example, unemployed people in one sector leads to a decrease in market tightness. This increases the probability of a vacancy being filled, which increases the value of the vacancy (see equation (6.3)). Because of free market entry, a corresponding number of vacancies will be offered, lowering market tightness to its original equilibrium value again. This also works when the number of unemployed people is decreased or vacancies are decreased and increased.

economy as well as the overall unemployment rate. Doing so after some rearranging yields

$$u^* = \frac{(1-\tilde{x})\theta^s q(\theta^s)(G(\epsilon_d^l)+\delta) + (\tilde{x}\theta^l q(\theta^l) + G(\epsilon_d^l)+\delta)(G(\epsilon_d^s)+\delta)}{[\lambda G(\epsilon_d^l) + \theta^l q(\theta^l) + \delta][\lambda G(\epsilon_d^s) + \theta^s q(\theta^s) + \delta]}. \tag{6.12}$$

6.3 Comparative Statics

6.3.1 Employment Protection, Education and Unemployment

It is straightforward to show that employed high-skilled workers benefit more from employment protection than low-skilled workers. For this to be the case, $\frac{d\epsilon_d^s}{dT} < \frac{d\epsilon_d^l}{dT}$ has to hold, which has already been shown by Guelfi (2004) and Kohns (2000) in a slightly different model framework. It can be easily shown that it also applies in this model (for a proof, see Appendix A.8). As we already know from the above analysis that high-skilled workers face a higher re-employment probability and shorter expected unemployment duration than low-skilled workers (resulting from $\theta^s > \theta^l$), the question of how an increase in employment protection changes the ex-ante decision of individuals on skill formation arises.

To show which effect a change in employment protection has on education, recall equation (6.10). Differentiating (6.10) with respect to firing costs T yields

$$\frac{d\tilde{x}}{dT} = \frac{\beta c}{(1-\beta)(r+\lambda)k}\left(\frac{d\theta^s}{dT} - \frac{d\theta^l}{dT}\right). \tag{6.13}$$

By totally differentiating the JD and JC, equations (6.8) and (6.9), we can derive

$$\frac{d\theta^i}{dT} = \frac{(1-\beta)\lambda G(\epsilon_d^i)}{(r+\delta+\lambda G(\epsilon_d^i))\frac{c}{q(\theta^i)^2}q'(\theta^i) - \beta c} < 0. \tag{6.14}$$

The change in market tightness due to a change in employment protection in both sectors differs in the original level of reservation productivity and market tightness. Increasing employment protection yields an increase in education if equation (6.13) is positive. This is the case only if $\frac{d\theta^l}{dT} < \frac{d\theta^s}{dT}$ holds, because the decrease in market tightness of the low-skilled must be greater than the one of the high-skilled. Using equation (6.13) in combination with equation (6.14) this is the case if (see Appendix A.9)

$$\left(\frac{G(\epsilon_d^l)}{G(\epsilon_d^s)}\frac{(r+\delta+\lambda G(\epsilon_d^s))}{(r+\delta+\lambda G(\epsilon_d^l))}+\beta\frac{G(\epsilon_d^l)-G(\epsilon_d^s)}{G(\epsilon_d^s)(r+\delta+\lambda G(\epsilon_d^l))}\frac{\theta^s q(\theta^s)}{\bar{\eta}}\right)>\frac{\theta^s q(\theta^s)}{\theta^l q(\theta^l)},\tag{6.15}$$

which after the exemption of β yields

$$\beta>\left(\frac{\theta^s q(\theta^s)}{\theta^l q(\theta^l)}-\frac{G(\epsilon_d^l)}{G(\epsilon_d^s)}\frac{(r+\delta+\lambda G(\epsilon_d^s))}{(r+\delta+\lambda G(\epsilon_d^l))}\right)\frac{G(\epsilon_d^s)(r+\delta+\lambda G(\epsilon_d^l))\bar{\eta}}{(G(\epsilon_d^l)-G(\epsilon_d^s))\theta^s q(\theta^s)}=\widehat{\beta},\tag{6.16}$$

where $0<\bar{\eta}=-\frac{q'(\theta^l)}{q(\theta^l)}\theta^l=-\frac{q'(\theta^s)}{q(\theta^s)}\theta^s<1$ for a Cobb-Douglas matching function.[7] Equation (6.16) states that as long as the bargaining power of workers exceeds some threshold value ($\beta>\widehat{\beta}$), education increases when employment protection is increased. The threshold value $\widehat{\beta}$ consists of the relative duration of unemployment between low- and high-skilled (first term in brackets) minus the relative dismissal probability between low- and high-skilled (second term in brackets). This is weighted by the relation between dismissal probabilities in the low- and high-skilled sector and the average unemployment duration in the high-skilled sector ($\frac{G(\epsilon_d^s)(r+\delta+\lambda G(\epsilon_d^l))}{\theta^s q(\theta^s)}$), as well as the relation of the differences of changes in market tightness and dismissal probabilities ($\frac{\bar{\eta}}{G(\epsilon_d^l)-G(\epsilon_d^s)}$).

The intuition is clear. The probability of finding a job in each sector decreases with each increase in employment protection. Obviously, it depends on the relative decrease of those probabilities. If the probability in the low-skilled sector decreases by more, it becomes relatively easier to find a job in the high-skilled sector. Therefore, more people get educated. The higher the bargaining power, the higher the worker's share of the surplus of a firm-worker-pair. If the bargaining power of workers is high enough

[7] If it was assumed that the matching functions differ in both sectors according to footnote 2 of this chapter, the first term in brackets of $\widehat{\beta}$, $\frac{\theta^s q(\theta^s)}{\theta^l q(\theta^l)}$, would have to be multiplied by σ. Furthermore, $\bar{\eta}$ would have to be replaced by $\eta^s=\alpha$. For $0<\sigma<1$, implying a better matching process in the high-skilled sector, the threshold value $\widehat{\beta}$ for workers to get more education decreases. Because of better matching in the high-skilled sector, market tightness relatively decreases even more in the low-skilled sector when employment protection is increased. This implies that workers will need to be less compensated for their investment in education. The opposite applies for a better matching process in the low-skilled sector, $\sigma>1$.

($\beta > \widehat{\beta}$), the worker obtains a sufficiently large fraction of the rent created by skill formation. In this case, therefore, more workers are willing to become educated.

It remains to be cleared why the fraction of educated workers increases with increasing employment protection under the condition that the bargaining power of workers exceeds a certain threshold value, $\hat{\beta}$, equation (6.16). It is straightforward to show by totally differentiating equations (6.8) and (6.9) with respect to β and following Appendix A.3 that

$$\frac{d\epsilon_d^i}{d\beta} = \frac{1}{D^i}\frac{c}{(1-\beta)}\left\{\beta\left[\frac{\epsilon_u - \epsilon_d^i}{r+\lambda} - T\right] - \bar{\eta}\frac{c}{q(\theta^i)}\right\} \tag{6.17}$$

where $D^i = \frac{r+\lambda G(\epsilon_d^i)}{r+\lambda}\frac{cq'(\theta^i)}{q(\theta^i)^2} - \frac{\beta c}{1-\beta} < 0$ and $\bar{\eta} = \eta^l = \eta^s$. We know form equation (6.9) that $\left[\frac{\epsilon_u - \epsilon_d^i}{r+\lambda} - T\right] > 0$. Hence, we see that an increase of the bargaining power of workers yields ambiguous effect on reservation productivity. As we know by the condition of Hosios (1990) that there is a socially optimal level of unemployment generated by an optimal level of bargaining power of workers (see chapter 4.4 or Pissarides 2000, p.189), this is not surprising. When the bargaining power is too low, there are not enough dismissals to generate the optimal level of unemployment as the firm's fraction of the job's surplus is high enough to avoid dismissals. The same holds for the bargaining power of workers being too high as then, workers do not agree upon the dismissal. Thus, the initial value of bargaining power of workers, β, determines whether reservation productivity increases or decreases when β is raised.

It can further be shown that market tightness decreases with increasing bargaining power,

$$\frac{d\theta^i}{d\beta} = \frac{1}{D^i}\frac{1}{(r+\lambda)}\left\{\frac{c\theta^i}{1-\beta} + [r+\lambda G(\epsilon_d^i)]\left[\frac{\epsilon_u - \epsilon_d^i}{r+\lambda} - T\right]\right\} < 0. \tag{6.18}$$

We further know from equation (6.9) that market tightness (i.e. job creation) increases with rising reservation productivity. With a low enough bargaining power of workers, β, reservation productivity could fall with an increase of β (see equation (6.17)). This reduces the decrease of market tightness. We can therefore conclude that the bargaining power of workers must be large enough to compensate for the dampening effect that a decrease of reservation productivity has on market tightness, as we know that the decline of market tightness in the low-skilled sector due to an increase of employment protection must exceed the corresponding decline of market tightness in the high-skilled sector for the level of eduction to increase. This is the case for $\beta > \hat{\beta}$.

It is straightforward to show that the fact that more workers get educated reduces unemployment. To prove this, we differentiate equation (6.12) with respect to k.

$$\frac{\partial u^*}{\partial k} = \frac{(G(\epsilon_d^s) + \delta)\theta^l q(\theta^l) - (G(\epsilon_d^l) + \delta)\theta^s q(\theta^s)}{(\lambda G(\epsilon_d^l) + \theta^l q(\theta^l) + \delta)(\lambda G(\epsilon_d^s) + \theta^s q(\theta^s) + \delta)} \frac{\partial \tilde{x}}{\partial k}, \tag{6.19}$$

where $\frac{\partial \tilde{x}}{\partial k} < 0$. Since it has already been demonstrated that $\epsilon_d^s < \epsilon_d^l$ and $\theta^s > \theta^l$, it is obvious that the first term on the right hand side, $\frac{\partial u^*}{\partial \tilde{x}}$, is negative. Therefore equation (6.19) is positive. Now decreasing education costs k increases the education level $\tilde{x}$ and therefore reduces unemployment.

The economic intuition is as follows. As can be seen in equation (6.11) in combination with (6.19) the unemployment rate in the high-skilled sector is lower than in the low-skilled sector. If more people move from the low-skilled sector to the high-skilled sector, less people are unemployed and therefore the overall unemployment rate falls.

Still, the effect of employment protection on overall unemployment is ambiguous since the effects on the unemployment rates in each sector are unclear, like in many existing publications (see Mortensen and Pissarides 2003). Employment protection leads to fewer dismissals, but at the same time to fewer vacancies, which implies fewer inflows into and fewer outflows out of unemployment. It is not clear which of the two effects is dominant.

In the present model, an additional effect is introduced. As has been shown above, education can be positively influenced by employment protection. Education in itself negatively influences the unemployment rate. Therefore, the effect of employment protection on unemployment differs through the educational channel from standard results. In case unemployment increases (decreases), this effect is weakened (boosted) by the negative effect education has on unemployment when employment protection is increased and $\beta > \widehat{\beta}$.

6.3.2 Calibration

To better assess the magnitude of the effects of employment protection on different skill groups and on the incentive to become skilled, we perform a simple calibration of the model. Following Mortensen and Pissarides (1999), we assume that the distribution of idiosyncratic productivity ϵ is uniform, here over $[-1, 1]$ and, therefore, $G(\epsilon) = \frac{1}{2}[1 + \epsilon]$ being the cumulative distribution function. Furthermore, $q(\theta^i) = (\theta^i)^{-\eta}$, with $0 < \eta < 1$. The values of the parameters are presented in Table 1 and intend to reflect the European case (Scenario 1) and the U.S. case (Scenario 2). Scenario 3 is added to show that the results also holds for other parametric specifications.

Parameter	Scenario 1 ($Sc.1$)	Scenario 2 ($Sc.2$)	Scenario 3 ($Sc.3$)
p	1.75	1.75	1.75
a^s	0.50	0.50	0.30
r	0.05	0.05	0.03
λ	0.70	0.30	0.30
c	0.30	0.30	0.30
β	0.50	0.50	0.50
δ	0.05	0.05	0.10
k	7.50	7.50	3.50
η	0.50	0.50	0.50

Table 6.1: Parameter Values in a Model with Education

The values are chosen to obtain an unemployment rate of about 8.8% for Europe (Scenario 1) and 6.5% for the US (Scenario 2) according to the actual employment report of the OECD (2004a) at an employment protection level $T = 0$. The resulting unemployment rate for Scenario 3 is 5.7%. Furthermore, the bargaining power is chosen to be $\beta = \eta$, according to the condition of Hosios (1990).[8] Broersma and van Ours (1999) find empirically that it is reasonable to assume $\eta = 0.5$. In all three scenarios, $\beta > \widehat{\beta}$ (see Figure 6.2). The above theoretical analysis predicts an increase in the level of education if employment protection is increased.

It is apparent from figure 6.1 that the level of education $\tilde{x}$ increases with employment protection T in all three scenarios as all three graphs have a positive slope.[9] That is because workers obtain a sufficiently large fraction of the investment in skill formation, since with these parameter constellations $\beta > \widehat{\beta}$ (as can be seen in figure 6.2) for all T that yield an economically reasonable solution for the unemployment rate.[10]

[8]The qualitative results of the above calibrations do not change if this is not the case. But following a standard assumption when calibrating matching models, this is assumed to hold here as well.

[9]The calibration allows for the speculation that a lower level of education costs, k, amplifies the increase of education as the slope of scenario 3 is much steeper than the one of scenarios 1 and 2.

[10]Economically reasonable solutions are those solutions where the unemployment rates do not fall below zero, which can be a mathematical solution in case $T > 0.85$.

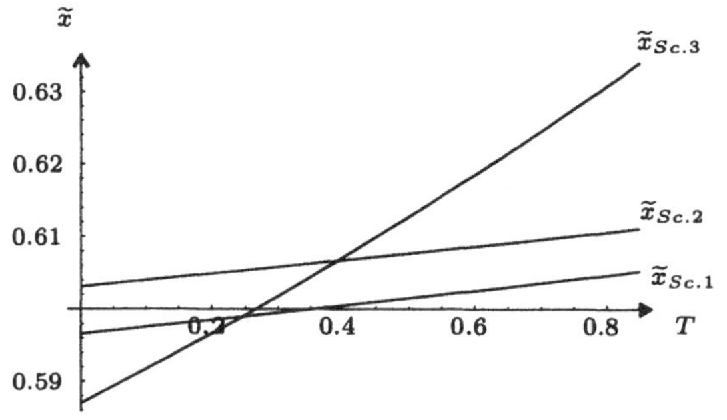

Figure 6.1: Education Level with Increasing Employment Protection

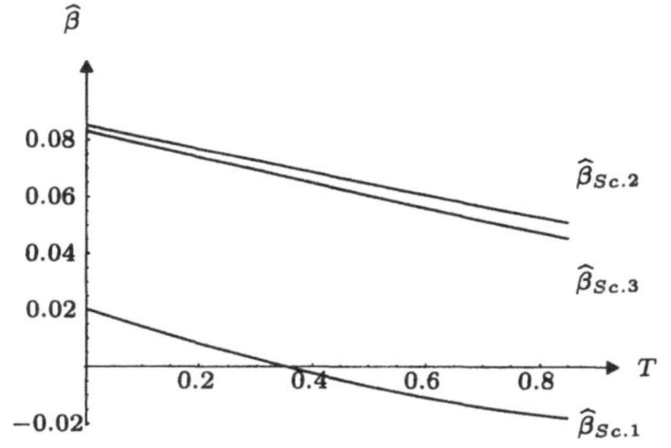

Figure 6.2: Threshold of Bargaining Power

Furthermore, using these parameter constellations, it can be shown that the levels of unemployment in both sectors and therefore in the entire economy fall when employment protection is increased. The simulation suggests that more employment protection can increase the level of education and decrease unemployment as long as the bargaining power of workers is great enough. However, as the negative effects on unemployment is driven by the functional and parametric specification, the graphs are not picture here to avoid the impression that more employment protection always decreases unemployment.

6.4 Extension One: Introducing Different Dismissal Costs

It is a reasonable assumption that dismissal costs in each skill-sector differ. We can imagine that it is more expensive to dismiss a high-skilled worker, as high-skilled workers might know more about their legal rights or can afford better lawyers to enforce those rights on the one hand. On the other hand, dismissal costs in the low-skilled sector could also be greater due to the government's will to protect disadvantaged workers. Employment protection must not necessarily be equal in both sectors. If we allow for dismissal costs to differ, this yields $T^s \neq T^l$. Firms then face different firing costs in each sector, which changes the corresponding firms' Bellman equations, equations (6.1) and (6.2), to

$$(r+\delta)J(\epsilon^i) = p+a^i+\epsilon^i-w(\epsilon^i)+\lambda\left[\int_{\epsilon_d^i}^{\epsilon_u} J(z)dG(z) + G(\epsilon_d^i)(-T^i) - J(\epsilon^i)\right] \tag{6.20}$$

and

$$(r+\delta)J^{0,i} = p+a^i+\epsilon_u^i-w^{0,i}+\lambda\left[\int_{\epsilon_d^i}^{\epsilon_u} J(x)dG(x) + G(\epsilon_d^i)(-T^i) - J^{0,i}\right]. \tag{6.21}$$

As pure firing costs do not influence the workers' utility functions, because they are "waste costs", workers' utility flows do not change and can be stated according to equations (6.5) to (6.7). Following the derivation of the job creation and job destruction condition according to section (6.2), we find them to be

$$p+a^i+\epsilon_d^i+\frac{\lambda}{r+\lambda+\delta}\int_{\epsilon_d^i}^{\epsilon_u}\left(z-\epsilon_d^i\right)dG(z) = \frac{\beta}{1-\beta}c\theta^i-(r+\delta)T^i \tag{6.22}$$

and

$$\frac{(1-\beta)\left(\epsilon_u-\epsilon_d^i\right)}{r+\lambda+\delta}-(1-\beta)T^i = \frac{c}{q(\theta^i)}. \tag{6.23}$$

For $T^s = T^l = T$, equations (6.22) and (6.23) are exactly the same as equations (6.8) and (6.9). Assuming that employment protection in the low-

(high-)skilled sector is greater yields $T^l > T^s$ ($T^s > T^l$). As we can easily see from equations (6.22) and (6.23), for the sector with higher employment protection ($T^i > T^j$, with $j = l, s$ and $i \neq j$), the JD and the JC decrease compared to the situation with equal employment protection, as presented in section 6.2. Therefore, the sector with a higher level of employment protection faces lower reservation productivity and lower market tightness.[11]

As the workers' utility stream is not directly influenced by the extension of different dismissal costs, the education decision is not changed either and can be displayed by equation (6.10). However, because sector-specific market tightness is changed, so is their relation. Hence, if firing costs in the low- (high-)skilled sector exceed those of the high- (low-)skilled sector, education increases (decreases). This is due to the fact that market tightness in the low- (high-)skilled sector then falls short of the market tightness of the initial situation in section 6.2.

Following the analysis of section 6.3 to investigate the effects of a simultaneous (and equal) increase of the level of employment protection, we find that

$$\frac{d\theta^i}{dT} = \frac{(1-\beta)\lambda G(\epsilon_d^i)}{(r+\delta+\lambda G(\epsilon_d^i))\frac{c}{q(\theta^i)^2}q'(\theta^i) - \beta c} < 0, \tag{6.24}$$

where $dT^s = dT^l = dT$. Equation (6.24) is exactly the same as equation (6.14). Therefore, the results of section 6.3 also apply if dismissal costs differ in each sector, as long as the increase of employment protection is the same. Hence, equations (6.13) and (6.16) also apply. It is obvious, though, that if $dT^s \neq dT^l$, market tightness decreases relatively more in the sector where the increase of firing costs is greater. This changes the education decision according to equation (6.13), yielding a higher increase of education if the increase of employment protection in the low-skilled sector exceeds the increase of the high-skilled sector and vice versa. The effects on unemployment are still ambiguous.

However, we are able to make an additional remark. If we assume that employment protection in the high-skilled sector is greater, the higher expected dismissal costs can overcompensate the productivity advantage over the low-skilled sector. This yields a lower (equal) market tightness in the

[11] We can easily prove this by referring to the analysis in section 6.3. There, we have shown that an increase of the level of employment protection T decreases sector-specific dismissals and job creation. Hence, if firing costs are increased in a single sector only, this sector faces fewer dismissals and less job creation than in the initial situation in section 6.2.

high-skilled sector, if

$$T^s - T^l < (=)\frac{a^s}{\lambda} + \frac{1-\beta}{r+\lambda}\left[\int_{\epsilon_d^s}^{\epsilon_u}(z-\epsilon_d^s)dG(z) - \int_{\epsilon_d^s}^{\epsilon_u}(z-\epsilon_d^l)dG(z)\right]$$

for equal idiosyncratic productivity ϵ in each sector. $\frac{a^s}{\lambda}$ results from the global productivity advantage and

$$\frac{1-\beta}{r+\lambda}\left[\int_{\epsilon_d^s}^{\epsilon_u}(z-\epsilon_d^s)dG(z) - \int_{\epsilon_d^s}^{\epsilon_u}(z-\epsilon_d^l)dG(z)\right]$$

results from the fact that reservation productivity, and therefore the option value in the case of a shock, differs in each sector.[12] This yields an education level $\tilde{x} = 0$ according to equation (6.10) which means that initially there will be no education. In this case, only a decrease (simultaneous or only in the high-skilled sector) of employment protection can result in more education.

6.5 Extension Two: Introducing Severance Payments

It seems also reasonable to assume that workers receive a severance payment S in case they are dismissed. We assume for simplicity that employment protection only consists of the severance payment and there are no additional firing costs. Further, we assume for comparability that $S = T$ which means that firms face the same costs through the severance payment as through pure firing costs in section 6.2 when laying off a worker. Therefore, the analysis of firms' behaviour can again be represented by equations (6.1) to (6.4). But now, in addition to the utility of unemployment, U^i, workers obtain a payment S in case they are fired, which re-writes their utility stream, equations (6.6) and (6.7), to

$$(r+\delta)W(\epsilon^i) = w(\epsilon^i) + \lambda\left[\int_{\epsilon_d^i}^{\epsilon_u} W(x)dG(x) + G(\epsilon_d^i)(U^i + S) - W(\epsilon^i)\right] \tag{6.25}$$

[12]The condition is simply derived by subtracting the low-skilled job value from the high-skilled job value, equations (6.20) and (6.21), and making use of $\int_{\epsilon_d^i}^{\epsilon_u} J(z)dG(z) = \frac{(1-\beta)}{r+\lambda}\int_{\epsilon_d^i}^{\epsilon_u}\left(z-\epsilon_d^i\right)dG(z) - T\int_{\epsilon_d^i}^{\epsilon_u} dG(z)$ (see Appendix A.2).

and

$$(r+\delta)W^{0,i} = w^{0,i}+\lambda\left[\int_{\epsilon_d^i}^{\epsilon_u} W(x)dG(x) + G(\epsilon_d^i)(U^i + S) - W^{0,i}\right]. \quad (6.26)$$

The wage bargaining between workers and firms is again modelled as a Nash bargaining game (see also Appendix A.1). Due to the severance payment, the threat point of workers in continuing jobs changes to $(U^i + S)$, while the one for continuing (newly created) firms stays at $-S$ ($V^i = 0$). The threat point of workers in newly created jobs stay at U^i as they are not eligible for a severance payment when the job is not created. This yields $w(\epsilon^i) = arg\ max\left(W(\epsilon) - (S + U^i)\right)^{\beta} \left(J(\epsilon) + S\right)^{1-\beta}$ for the wage of continuing jobs and $w^{0,i} = argmax\left(W^0 - U^i\right)^{\beta} J^{0,i\,1-\beta}$ for newly created jobs. Wages then turn out to be

$$w(\epsilon^i) = \beta[p + a^i + \epsilon^i + (r+\delta)S + c\theta^i] + (1-\beta)(r+\delta)S \quad (6.27)$$

and

$$w^{0,i} = \beta[p+a^i+\epsilon_u - \lambda S + c\theta^i] - (1-\beta)\lambda S = w(\epsilon_u) - (r+\lambda+\delta)S. \quad (6.28)$$

By comparing these wages, equations (6.27) and (6.28), with the wages resulting in section 6.2, $w(\epsilon^i) = \beta[p + a^i + \epsilon^i + (r+\delta)T + c\theta^i]$ and $w^{0,i} = \beta[p + a^i + \epsilon_u - \lambda T + c\theta^i] = w(\epsilon_u) - \beta(r+\delta+\lambda)T$, respectively, we see that the wage of continuing job increases by $(1-\beta)(r+\delta)S$, whereas the wage of newly created jobs decreases by $(1-\beta)\lambda S$ for $S = T$. Hence, if employment protection is modeled as severance pay, insider wages increase and outsider wages decrease. This can easily be explained by the bargaining process. As the severance payment is a transfer from firms to workers who are dismissed, the worker initially bargaining over wages accepts a lower wage for the job to be created (modeled by the reduced threat point). He regains this initial loss through higher wages when bargaining after a shock.

Using the wages resulting from the presence of severance payments, equations (6.27) and (6.28), to derive the JD and the JC (following Appendix A.2), we get

$$\epsilon_d^i + \frac{\lambda}{r+\lambda+\delta}\int_{\epsilon_d^i}^{\epsilon_u}\left(z - \epsilon_d^i\right) dG(z) = \frac{\beta}{1-\beta}c\theta^i \quad (6.29)$$

as the JD and

$$\frac{(1-\beta)(\epsilon_u - \epsilon_d^i)}{r+\lambda+\delta} = \frac{c}{q(\theta^i)} \quad (6.30)$$

as JC.

Again, equations (6.29) and (6.30) simultaneously determine the equilibrium values for reservation productivity ϵ_d^i and market tightness θ^i in each sector. Comparing job destruction and job creation in the presence of severance payments to the equivalent conditions in the presence of pure firing costs, equations (6.8) and (6.9), we see that severance payments do not influence the job creation and job destruction decision of workers (as S does not appear in equations (6.29) and (6.30)). This confirms the classical neutrality result of Lazear (1990) already mentioned in matching models.

The reasoning is quite straightforward. By the wage reduction in the bargains for newly created jobs, described in equation (6.28), the firm makes the worker repay the severance payment entirely. The wage is diminished by the amount λS every period and this will last on average $1/\lambda$. We could consider the wage reduction, λS, as some sort of deposit made by the worker. After the job has been formed, the worker becomes an insider and, because of the increased threat point, earns interest upon the deposit held by the firm. Upon separation, the worker receives his deposit back. In total, this has no allocative effect (given risk neutrality). For a more detailed analysis dealing with the effects of severance payments in matching models, incorporating unionised wage bargaining and bargaining restrictions, see also Garibaldi and Violante (2005).

To summarise the findings of this extension, we have seen that when employment protection is modelled as a severance payment, there are no effects on job creation when those are increased. Hence, there are no educational effects. Stähler (2006) claims in his conclusion that it would not matter if employment protection was modelled as pure firing costs or as severance payments (without giving a detailed proof). We have shown that this is not true, as severance payments have no allocative effects.

6.6 Conclusion

The main result of this chapter is that more employment protection increases the level of education acquired by workers ex-ante as long as workers obtain a sufficiently large fraction of the rent resulting from skill formation. This is due to the fact that increasing employment protection relatively increases the (re-)employment chances of high-skilled workers through market tightness. In addition to the better re-employment chances of high-skilled workers, it can be shown that high-skilled workers get dismissed later than low-skilled workers and benefit more from an increase in employment protection. Furthermore, a higher level of education unambiguously decreases unemployment.

Qualitatively, it does not matter if dismissal costs differ in each sector. However, we have shown that if employment protection is modelled as severance payment, there are no allocative effects due to the well-known neutrality result of Lazear (1990). Hence, there is no change in the level of education when severance payments are increased. While the findings about sector-specific dismissal costs is in line with Stähler (2006), our findings of severance payments contradict the claim by Stähler (2006) that such a modelling would not change the results qualitatively. The proof of this claim is, however, missing. We therefore think that our findings are correct and conclude that severance payments do not alter the level of education in the matching framework presented here.

This chapter complements Burda (2003) and Wasmer (2003). In their works, they suggest that education is achieved "on-the-job". While Burda (2003) finds that more employment protection decreases education, Wasmer (2003) finds the opposite. This is due to the fact that in the model presented by Burda (2003), the firm bears the costs of education, while in the model by Wasmer (2003), the worker faces those costs. Next to the fact that it is important who pays for education, we introduce a novel argument to the discussion. It is not only important who pays for education, but also when the education decision takes place. As a huge part of workers' skill formation happens before they enter the labour market (OECD 2004b), this is an interesting topic to think about. Despite the fact that it might seem odd to use employment protection as an instrument to increase education, we have seen that education can be increased by more employment protection under the above mentioned conditions. Especially for developed countries, this argument might be interesting, as it is often claimed that in times of globalisation comparative advantages can only be maintained through greater innovation and well educated workers. We can additionally conclude that high levels of bargaining power amongst workers have positive effects on their education decision. Therefore, relatively high levels of workers' bargaining power and employment protection might be one of the influencing factors for education.

Nevertheless, the results should not be misinterpreted as a pleading for more employment protection. As we have also seen, the ambiguous effects that an increase of employment protection have on overall unemployment cannot be resolved.

Chapter 7

Employment Protection in a Unionised Economy with Search Frictions

7.1 Introduction

From a theoretical point of view, the effects of employment protection on unemployment are ambiguous. Stronger dismissal protection indeed decreases dismissals, but decreases job creation at the same time, as employers will take into account the likelihood that firing costs will be incurred in the future in their decision whether to hire a new worker (Mortensen and Pissarides 1999). Empirical studies confirm this ambiguity (OECD 2004a). It has to be considered, however, that many former scientific findings about the effects of employment protection on unemployment are only suitable to characterise the continental European labour market to a limited extent. In most works, the labour market structure is assumed to be of an Anglo-Saxon type, where workers and firms bargain more or less individually over wages (see, e.g., Guelfi 2004, Mortensen and Pissarides 1999 and 2003, and Pissarides 2001, just to mention a few). But the labour market structure of many European countries is characterised by a high degree of collective bargaining power of workers (e.g., through unionisation), as can easily be confirmed by the OECD (OECD 2004a).

The modeling of unionised wage bargaining in combination with employment protection has hardly been covered in the existing literature due to problems that are made obvious in the model by Booth (1995b). Nevertheless, they can be overcome by introducing collective bargaining into search models. Indeed, the initial search models in the manner of Mortensen and Pissarides (1994) reproduce the Anglo-Saxon labour market structure. However, Mortensen and Pissarides (1999) highlight the possibility to introduce different wage bargaining schemes into the "classical" search model where workers and firms bargain individually over wages. They integrate strategic bilateral bargaining, insider wages, efficiency wages, and, most important for our purpose, union wages set by a monopoly union. They introduce a monopoly union which sets the wage that firms take as given and determine employment. In their framework, the union represents employed workers and is assumed to be a democracy. The employed median voter (who is the one with the median match product) is the one that is relevant for wage determination. The resulting wage is similar to the one where firms and workers bargain individually, except that it does not depend on the individual productivity of a firm-worker-pair, but on the median match product. Therefore, the introduction of employment protection also generates similar effects on unemployment as already found in literature with individual wage bargaining (see, e.g., Mortensen and Pissarides 2003). Also, Garibaldi and Violante (2005) use the median voter approach to introduce unions into matching models. A utilitarian union is presented as an extension. However, the utilitarian union only takes into account the utility of employed workers. The new effect introduced by this kind of modeling is that now the wage set by the utilitarian union is lower than the one set by the median voter union. This is due to the fact that the utilitarian union takes into consideration that high wages displace more workers.

We introduce firms that employ more than one worker, following the approach of Pissarides (2000), and firm-specific, utilitarian unions that set wages. Unions also consider the utility of unemployed members. Firms take the wage set by unions as given and then determine employment. When increasing employment protection, marginal labour costs increase from the firms' point of view. This makes firms decrease employment and, as this holds for all firms, market tightness decreases. Hence, re-employment chances for unemployed workers decrease as well. Decreasing re-employment chance reduces the unions' wage claim, while a lower employment level increases the wage claim. If the wage drop through lower re-employment chances dominates the wage increase of lower firm-specific employment, the total wage claim decreases. But even if this condition holds, the lower wage costs cannot compensate the higher dismissal costs. Therefore, in a unionised economy, unemployment unambiguously increases when employment protection is increased. Additionally, the chapter shows that the reduction of employment and market tightness with a unionised wage setting differs from the reduction of employment and market tightness with full exogenous wage rigidity, confirming Garibaldi and Violante (2005). If the reduction of the unions' wage claim due to lower market tightness exceeds the increase of the unions' wage claim due to a decreased level of employment, the decrease of market tightness and employment with full wage rigidity exceeds the decrease in the presence of unionisation. Otherwise, it is stronger in the case of full wage rigidity.

It should be noted that the analysis presented beneath is indeed driven by arguable assumptions. The present chapter, however, contributes two important features. First, we allow for an alternative approach of unionised wage bargaining with firms employing more than one worker. Within this framework, we are able to approve that, regarding employment protection, pure firing costs and severance payments act qualitatively different, as already pointed out by Garibaldi and Violante (2005). Secondly and maybe more importantly, it is shown that the labour market effects due to employment protection crucially depend on the wage bargaining structure.

The chapter is organized as follows. Section 7.2 describes the model. In section 7.3, the analysis is performed. In section 7.4, the main results are summarized.

7.2 The Model

7.2.1 Basic Structure

The world is populated by a mass of workers set to unity. Firms are perfectly symmetric within the economy. Time is continuous. Each individual firm's output is produced according to the production function $F(n_i)$ with positive but decreasing returns to labour, n_i, which is the sole input factor. Firms decide on the number of workers by supplying vacancies V_i. Each vacancy costs c per unit of time. Output prices are normalized to unity.

Following Pissarides (2000), the labour market is characterized by search frictions. Only unemployed workers search for jobs. Job-seeking takes time, and unemployment and vacancies exist at the same time. The matching process is described by a linear homogeneous and concave matching function $m(v, u)$, where u is the unemployment rate and v the vacancy rate of the economy. The ratio $\theta = v/u$ is called market tightness. It is determined endogenously. The rate at which vacancies are filled is given by $q(\theta) = m(1/\theta, 1)$, where $q'(\theta) < 0$. Unemployed workers find a job at rate $\theta q(\theta) =$

$m(\theta, 1)$, where $[\theta q(\theta)]' > 0$. We assume that individual firms are small and take market tightness θ as given. It is later on determined in equilibrium.

Productivity shocks exist which occur to every worker at the Poisson rate λ. In the case of a shock, the employment relationship is destroyed, in which case the firm has to pay a dismissal cost, T. Furthermore, firms have to pay a severance payment γT with $\gamma \geq 0$ to the worker when laying him off. Note that for $\gamma = 0$, we find ourselves in a situation without severance payments. It should be noted that as soon as the shock λ occurs, the job is destroyed with certainty and no endogenous job destruction exists. Therefore, λ represents worker-specific shocks that make the worker unproductive from the firms' point of view and, thus, the firm lays the worker off (which cannot be done without cost). Examples for such shocks would be illness, personal dismissal reasons, etc. λ does not necessarily represent an operational shock. This combination, a shock which certainly destroys the job and forces the firm to pay some dismissal costs, is done for tractability reasons. It is, nevertheless going to drive our results. However, this modeling is common in literature dealing with employment protection an unionised wage setting (see Booth 1995b or Belot and van Ours 2004, for example).

Workers can be either employed or unemployed. If employed, they receive utility of the wage they earn and face the probability of getting dismissed. For simplicity, there are no unemployment benefits. Therefore, unemployed workers only obtain the utility of the option value of finding an employment. Wages are set by firm specific, utilitarian unions. Unions are interested in the wage of the employed, w_i, the employment level of their members, n_i, and the utility of unemployed workers. Therefore, they bear in mind the firm's reaction of their wage setting. The union set wage is taken as given by the firms. Firms then set the level of employment and decide on their number of vacancies. This is the so-called "right-to-manage" model (see, e.g., Booth, 1995a).

In what follows we will describe the model in more detail. First, we will determine individuals firm's employment decision. Second, we focus on the union's utility function. And last, we are going to derive the equilibrium conditions as well as the equilibrium unemployment rate.

7.2.2 The Value Functions and Wages

Firms

Each firm maximises its profit, π_i, by deciding on the level of employment, n_i, which it can influence by the offer of firm-specific vacancies, V_i. Firms take wages, w_i, as given. In the case they dismiss a worker, which occurs with probability λ, they have to pay dismissal costs $(1+\gamma)T$. Each firm's profit over time, t, can therefore be written as

$$\pi_i = \int_0^\infty e^{-rt}\{(F(n_i) - w_i n_i - \lambda n_i(1+\gamma)T - cV_i\}\, dt. \tag{7.1}$$

The profit, equation (7.1), is maximised with respect to the number of vacancies, V_i and the level of employment, n_i subject to

$$\dot{n_i} = q(\theta)V_i - \lambda n_i, \tag{7.2}$$

where equation (7.2) represents the change of employment over time. Employment increases according to new vacancies which are filled at rate $q(\theta)$ and decreases according to dismissals that occur with probability λ. Remember that market tightness, θ, is given from the individual firm's perspective. Solving the dynamic maximising problem, described in equations (7.1) and (7.2), yields (for calculations, see Appendix A.10)

$$F'(n_i) = w_i + \lambda(1+\gamma)T + (r+\lambda)\frac{c}{q(\theta)}. \tag{7.3}$$

The left hand side of equation (7.3) is the marginal product of labour, whereas the right hand side represents the marginal cost of labour. Those costs consist of the wage that has to be paid, w_i, the expected marginal dismissal costs, $\lambda(1+\gamma)T$, and the compounded marginal search costs, $(r+\lambda)\frac{c}{q(\theta)}$.

Workers and Unions

As already mentioned, each worker can be either employed or unemployed. Unemployed workers get utility from the probability of finding a job and can, therefore, be represented by the Bellman equation

$$rU = \theta q(\theta)[W_i - U], \tag{7.4}$$

where W_i is the utility of the worker employed at firm i. When employed, the worker receives utility from his wage income w_i per period and faces the probability of a job loss, λ, which generates the utility loss $[U - W_i]$. In the case of a dismissal, the worker obtains a severance payment γT. This can be expressed by the Bellman equation

$$rW_i = w_i + \lambda[U - W_i + \gamma T]. \tag{7.5}$$

Following Mortensen and Pissarides (1999), only unemployed workers search for jobs.

Each firm-specific utilitarian union considers the utility of their employed members, n_iW_i, and $(1 - [n_i + \sum n_j]) U$, the utility of all unemployed workers, where $\sum n_j$ are those workers not employed at firm i and, therefore, are not in the sphere of union i.[1] The unions' utility function can be expressed as

$$\Omega_i = n_iW_i + \left(1 - [n_i + \sum n_j]\right) U. \tag{7.6}$$

Wage Setting

The firm-specific union maximises its utility, equation (7.6), with respect to n_i and w_i subject to equation (7.3), which represents the firm's reaction to the wage setting. The wage that is set by this union calculates as (for calculations, see Appendix A.11)

$$w_i = rU - \lambda\gamma T - n_iF''(n_i). \tag{7.7}$$

As can be seen in equation (7.7), the wage consists of the utility stream of not working, rU, - which is the alternative income -, plus some positive extra charge for working, $-n_iF''(n_i) > 0$, which is quite a standard result for unionised wage setting. The severance payment γT that a worker receives in the case of a dismissal decreases the wage claim of the union and can be interpreted in analogy to Lazear (1990) as a "belated wage payment", where workers get a compensation in the case of a job loss and, therefore, accept lower wages. The wage set by the unions therefore positively depends on the alternative income U (which itself positively depends on the re-employment chances for unemployed) and negatively on the employment level within the firm, n_i, as well as negatively on the severance payment.[2]

7.2.3 Job Creation, Unemployment and Equilibrium

In steady state, the change of employment, $\dot{n}_i$, is equal to zero. From equation (7.2) we therefore get

$$V_i = \frac{\lambda n_i}{q(\theta)}, \tag{7.8}$$

[1] Note that the unions are assumed to not only care about the utility of their employed members, n_iW_i, but also of the utility of all unemployed workers, $(1-[n_i+\sum n_j])U$. The reason for assuming this is that this is claimed publicly by union officials. Unemployed workers are counted by each union.

[2] Note that $\frac{dw_i}{dn_i} = -[F''(n_i) + n_iF'''(n_i)] < 0$.

as the steady state solution for the individual firm's vacancies. Because of perfectly symmetrical firms, equation (7.8) states that all firms choose the same ratio of vacancies to employment in steady state and, therefore, it also gives the economy wide ratio of vacancies to total employment (see Pissarides 2000). As the total number of workers is normalised to unity, we can express $\sum_i V_i = v = \theta u$ and $\sum_i n_i = (1-u)$. Inserting this into equation (7.8) implies $\theta \frac{u}{(1-u)} = \frac{\lambda}{q(\theta)}$ which after rearranging gives

$$u = \frac{\lambda}{\lambda + \theta q(\theta)}. \tag{7.9}$$

As population is normalised to unity, $u = (1-n)$. With full exogenous wage rigidity, equations (7.3) and (7.9) simultaneously determine the equilibrium values for market tightness, θ, and employment, $n_i = n$, for $w_i = \bar{w}$. Thus, they also determine the unemployment rate u. For unionised wage bargaining, we find the following.

As all firms are perfectly symmetrical, we can express

$$rU = \theta q(\theta) \frac{w + \lambda\gamma T}{[r + \lambda + \theta q(\theta)]}$$

after combining equations (7.4) and (7.5), where $w = w_i$ for all i. Substituting this into the wage set by each single union, we can express the aggregated wage as

$$w = -\frac{r + \lambda + \theta q(\theta)}{r + \lambda} n F''(n) - \lambda\gamma T, \tag{7.10}$$

where the omission of the index i indicates that it is the same for all firms and, therefore, holds on an aggregate level (which shall hold henceforth). Again, we see that it positively depends on market tightness, θ, and negatively on employment, n, as well as negatively on the severance payment, γT. After inserting the aggregated wage, equation (7.10), into the individual firm's labour demand function, equation (7.3), total labour demand is given by

$$F'(n) = -\frac{r + \lambda + \theta q(\theta)}{r + \lambda} n F''(n) + \lambda T + (r + \lambda)\frac{c}{q(\theta)}. \tag{7.11}$$

Equation (7.11) also results for the case of no severance payments, $\gamma = 0$. That is because severance payments decrease the wage claim by unions according to equations (7.7) and (7.10) and are therefore neutral for employment as claimed by Lazear (1990). We can therefore confirm the result of Garibaldi and Violante (2005), stating that pure firing costs and severance payments are qualitatively different in the presence of unionised wage bargaining. As severance payments do not influence equilibrium in this setting, for the following analysis, we assume that $\gamma = 0$.

Note that due to the fact that union wages decrease with increasing employment (see equation (7.10)), there is the possibility of multiple equilibria as can be seen in figure 7.1. Employment (unemployment) unambiguously increases (decreases) with increasing market tightness according to equation (7.9). Therefore, equation (7.9) can be depicted as a constantly upward sloping curve in an employment market tightness space ($n-\theta$-space).[3] Equation (7.11) is the equilibrium labour demand. An increase of market tightness increases search and wage costs. This increase of costs results in two incentives for the firm. On the one hand, to employ less workers as this increases the marginal product of labour. On the other hand, to employ more workers, as this results in lower wage costs. Therefore, the labour demand curve can be both negatively and positively sloped. A necessary and sufficient condition for it to be positively sloped is $nF'''(n) > -[1 + \frac{\theta q(\theta)}{r+\lambda+\theta q(\theta)}]F''(n)$.[4] In this case, additional costs resulting from an increase of market tightness can be overcompensated by a decrease of wage costs by in turn increasing employment.

7.3 Comparative Statics

For clarification, we start off by analysing the increase of employment protection T by assuming that we have full exogenous wage rigidity as a reference case. This is in analogy to Garibaldi and Violante (2005). We are unambiguously on the downward sloping part of the labour demand curve in figure 7.1. Assuming full exogenous wage rigidity for the moment, the wage is $w_i = \bar{w}$. The following analysis is straightforward. An increase of employment protection increases labour costs, which implies less employment and lower market tightness. Graphically, the labour demand curve

[3] As the matching function $m(u, v)$ is assumed to be linear homogeneous with a positive but decreasing marginal product in each argument, u and v, $\theta q(\theta)$ is positively, but decreasingly dependent on θ.

[4] Note that the labour demand curve does not necessarily have the form shown in figure 7.1. It is an exemplary form where $F(n_i) = n_i^{\alpha}$, with $0 < \alpha < 1$. Nevertheless, the different equilibria can be distinguished by their property of being on the upward or downward sloping part of the labour demand curve.

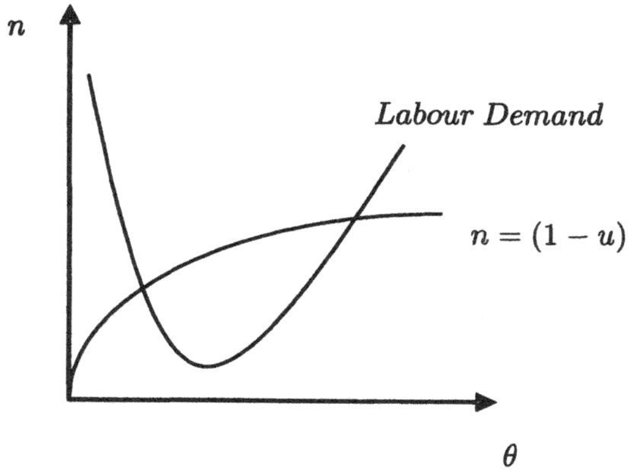

Figure 7.1: Possible Multiple Equilibria with Unionised Wage Bargaining

shifts down. Thus, with exogenous wage rigidity (which could be, e.g., a legal minimum wage), employment protection increases unemployment (see, e.g., Garibaldi and Violante 2005). Formally, we see that for $w_i = \bar{w}$ being the exogenous wage, an increase of employment protection T yields (from totally differentiating equations (7.3) and (7.9))

$$\frac{dn}{dT} = \frac{1}{\widetilde{D}} \frac{q(\theta)[1-\eta(\theta)]\lambda^2}{(\lambda+\theta q(\theta))^2} < 0, \tag{7.12}$$

and

$$\frac{d\theta}{dT} = \frac{1}{\widetilde{D}}\lambda < 0, \tag{7.13}$$

where

$$\widetilde{D} = F''(n)\frac{q(\theta)[1-\eta(\theta)]\lambda}{(\lambda+\theta q(\theta))^2} + (r+\lambda)\frac{cq'(\theta)}{q(\theta)^2} < 0, \tag{7.14}$$

where $0 < \eta(\theta) = -\frac{\theta q'(\theta)}{q(\theta)} < 1$.

With endogenous wage rigidity, resulting from the unionised wage setting, there is a negative feedback between employment and union wages. Again, we see that the labour demand curve shifts down in figure 7.1 due to an increase of employment protection, T. But now, we have the possibility of being on either part of the labour demand curve (the downward and upward sloping part). In the following, the employment effects of an increase of dismissal costs are dissected. We restrict our attention to the steady state. Totally differentiating equations (7.11) and (7.9) yields (for calculations, see Appendix A.12)

$$\frac{dn}{dT} = \frac{1}{D} \frac{q(\theta)[1-\eta(\theta)]\lambda^2}{(\lambda + \theta q(\theta))^2}, \tag{7.15}$$

and

$$\frac{d\theta}{dT} = \frac{1}{D}\lambda, \tag{7.16}$$

where

$$\begin{aligned} D &= \left\{ F''(n) + \frac{r+\lambda+\theta q(\theta)}{r+\lambda} \left[F''(n) + nF'''(n)\right] \right\} \frac{q(\theta)[1-\eta(\theta)]\lambda}{(\lambda+\theta q(\theta))^2} \\ &+ \left\{ (r+\lambda)\frac{cq'(\theta)}{q(\theta)^2} + \frac{nF''(n)q(\theta)(1-\eta(\theta))}{r+\lambda} \right\}. \end{aligned} \tag{7.17}$$

As can easily be seen in equations (7.15) and (7.16), the effect of an increase of employment protection T on market tightness θ and the employment level n depends on the sign of D. Equation (7.17) states that it is ambiguous. If $D > 0$, then employment and market tightness increase when increasing employment protection T. The opposite holds for $D < 0$. On the downward sloping part of the labour demand curve of figure 7.1, $D < 0$, as $F''(n) + \frac{r+\lambda+\theta q(\theta)}{r+\lambda}[F''(n) + nF'''(n)]$. Therefore, $D > 0$ is possible only on the upward sloping part of the labour demand curve.

As D is the determinant of the Jakobi matrix of the system of equations (7.9) and (7.11), we are able conclude that the equilibrium on the downward sloping part of the labour demand curve is stable, as $D < 0$. For the case that $D > 0$ (only possible on the upward sloping part of the labour demand curve), we see that

$$\left\{ F''(n) + \frac{r+\lambda+\theta q(\theta)}{r+\lambda}\left[F''(n) + nF'''(n)\right] \right\} + \frac{q(\theta)[1-\eta(\theta)]\lambda}{(\lambda+\theta q(\theta))^2} < 0$$

has to hold for the equilibrium to be stable. As both parts of the left hand side of this equation are positive on the upward sloping part of the labour demand curve, the equilibrium there is not stable. In the following, we will restrict our analysis to the stable equilibrium.

Therefore, $D < 0$. We then see from equations (7.15) to (7.17) that employment and market tightness unambiguously decrease when increasing employment protection. An increase of firing costs, T, increases expected labour costs. Therefore, firms reduce employment. This reduction of employment decreases market tightness as all firms act the same way. Reduced market tightness decreases the unions' wage claim, while reduced employment increases the wage claim. Even when the total wage claim is decreased, it cannot compensate the additional dismissal costs. Hence, unemployment increases. But what is the difference to the case with exogenous wage rigidity?

As we know that $\widetilde{D}, D < 0$, we see from equations (7.12), (7.13), (7.15) and (7.16) that the decrease of employment and market tightness is greater in the case of full exogenous wage rigidity ($w = \bar{w}$) if $D < \widetilde{D}$. Subtracting equation (7.14) from (7.17) this is the case if

$$\frac{r+\lambda+\theta q(\theta)}{r+\lambda}\left[F''(n)+nF'''(n)\right]\frac{q(\theta)[1-\eta(\theta)]\lambda}{(\lambda+\theta q(\theta))^2} + \frac{nF''(n)q(\theta)(1-\eta(\theta))}{r+\lambda} < 0. \tag{7.18}$$

Re-writing equation (7.18) allows us to state that this is the case if

$$\frac{dw}{d\theta} > -\frac{dw}{dn}\frac{dn}{d\theta},$$

where

$$\frac{dw}{d\theta} = -\frac{q(\theta)(1-\eta(\theta)}{r+\lambda}nF''(n) > 0,$$

$$\frac{dw}{dn} = -\frac{r+\lambda+\theta q(\theta)}{r+\lambda}\left[F''(n)+nF'''(n)\right] < 0$$

and

$$\frac{dn}{d\theta} = \frac{q(\theta)[1-\eta(\theta)]\lambda}{(\lambda+\theta q(\theta))^2} > 0$$

which can be confirmed by equations (7.10) and (7.9). Otherwise, the decrease of employment and market tightness is bigger in the case with endogenous wage rigidity due to unionisation.

Due to a change of employment protection and the resulting decrease of employment, in both cases, with exogenous and endogenous wage rigidity, the increase of marginal search costs, $(r+\lambda)\frac{cq'(\theta)}{q(\theta)^2} < 0$ resulting from a decrease of market tightness, θ, is equal. But in the case with unionised wage setting, the reduction of market tightness and employment has some additional effects (see equation (7.10)). On the one hand, due to reduced market tightness and, therefore, lower re-employment chances of unemployed workers, the wage claim of unions decreases ($\frac{dw}{d\theta}$). On the other hand, due to reduced employment within one firm, the wage claim of unions increases ($\frac{dw}{dn}\frac{dn}{d\theta}$).

If the wage reduction induced by a decrease of market tightness is greater than the wage increase induced by a decrease of the employment level ($\frac{dw}{d\theta} > -\frac{dw}{dn}\frac{dn}{d\theta}$), the total wage claim of unions decreases. This decreases the increase of marginal labour costs and, therefore, boosts employment. The opposite holds if the decrease of the unions' wage claim due to a reduction of market tightness is smaller than the increase of the wage claim resulting from lower employment. In the case of full exogenous wage rigidity, there is not going to be a change in wages.

7.4 Conclusion

The present chapter does two important things. First of all, it incorporates unionised wage bargaining into matching models, where firms employ more than one worker and unions also consider the utility of their unemployed members. This is a new development in search models, as the introduction of unions has mainly been done for unions that only consider the utility of their employed members (see Mortensen and Pissarides 1999 and Garibaldi and Violante 2005). Second, it contributes to the discussion of employment protection in a unionised economy with search frictions. It has been shown that an increase of employment protection decreases employment and market tightness, and therefore re-employment chances for unemployed workers. This is due to the fact that an increase of employment protection results in an increase of marginal labour costs that cannot be compensated by a possible decrease of unions' wage claims due to lower employment and lower re-employment chances of unemployed workers.

Additionally, the chapter shows that the reduction of employment and market tightness with a unionised wage setting differs from the reduction of employment and market tightness with exogenous wage rigidity. In the case of unionised wage setting, the decrease of employment and market tightness falls short of the decrease of employment and market tightness in the case of fully exogenous wage rigidity, if the reduction of the unions' wage claim due to lower market tightness exceeds the increase of the unions' wage claim due to a decreased level of employment. This is because then, wages are reduced. The opposite holds if the reduction of the unions' wage claim due to lower market tightness is smaller than the increase of the unions' wage claim due to a decreased level of employment

Nevertheless, this chapter also shows that further research will be needed concerning employment protection in unionised economies. From a theoretical point of view, it has to be mentioned that we have only looked at a special form of employment protection, namely, the protection of workers that are hit by a shock themselves (as, for instance, maternity protection, sick leave protection, etc.). General shocks that hit the entire economy should be subject of further inquiries. Furthermore, we have considered perfectly symmetrical firms and unions, as well as homogeneous and risk neutral workers. Changing these assumptions might lead to different results.

Chapter 8

Conclusion

In this work, we address the question of how employment protection affects unemployment. We give an overview about the dimensions of employment protection, defining what it actually is and how it is integrated into theoretical economic models. A brief overview of those regulations of dismissal protection that the analysis is focused on is given for Germany. Further, we provide an overview of labour market models and the development of the recently most accepted labour market model, namely the search and matching model. We additionally give an insight into the recent economic literature dealing with employment protection. The core of our work is the theoretical analysis evaluating recent policy proposals that are discussed in Europe. It is mainly a positive analysis describing the effects of employment protection on unemployment. First, we discuss the effects of an experience rated unemployment insurance. Second, we discuss the difference of pure firing costs and severance payments in the presence of judicial mistakes. Third, we analyse the effects employment protection has on the ex-ante skill formation of workers. Last, we concentrate on the effects employment protection has in unionised economies with search frictions. This chapter provides a summary of the results. The effects at work are discussed in more detail in the conclusions of the corresponding chapters. However, in this chapter, we also discuss the political implications of our results.

Financing unemployment benefits through dismissal taxes reduces the externality of financing unemployment insurance through employment contributions. The introduction of dismissal taxes therefore decreases the total tax burden that firms face from financing the insurance. Hence, changing the system toward a system of experience rating can indeed decrease unemployment. This is the case as long as dismissal taxes do not yet cover the average costs of an unemployed worker and the unemployment insurance itself is on the increasing part of the Laffer curve regarding contributions of employment taxes. Our results suggest that an experience rated unemployment insurance is desirable if policy aims at a reduction of unemployment.

The discussion about severance payments in the presence of judicial mistakes has shown that an increase of the level of severance payment can unambiguously increase employment if judicial mistakes are small. In this case, severance payments unambiguously dominate pure firing costs in fighting unemployment. The opposite holds for very large judicial mistakes. Judicial mistakes themselves increase unemployment. As there is no robust empirical finding about the magnitude of judicial mistakes, the results of our analysis clearly suggest that empirical research should aim at estimating how large judicial mistakes actually are. Based on our analysis, we cannot give any policy advice on how to reduce unemployment without knowing how large those mistakes are.

We have also shown that employment protection increases the incentive for ex-ante skill formation as long as workers obtain a sufficiently large fraction of the rent created through education. Higher education of the population clearly decreases unemployment. Nevertheless, as employment protection not only increases the incentive for education, but also decreases the firms' incentive for job creation, the overall effects of an increase of employment protection on unemployment remain ambiguous in our analysis, even when allowing for different levels of skills (where more education itself decreases unemployment).

If the economy is characterised by a high degree of unionisation, our analysis shows that employment protection decreases employment. This is due to the fact that even though, when the unions' wage claim decreases with increasing employment protection through more job security and lower re-employment chances, this effect cannot compensate the additional costs that firms face through higher employment protection. Hence, our analysis suggests that in a unionised economy, employment protection, neither modelled as pure firing costs nor modelled as severance payments, seems to be an appropriate mean to reduce unemployment.

We can therefore conclude from our analysis that employment protection has ambiguous effects on unemployment. It highly depends on the labour market structure, i.e., the wage bargaining structure, and on the design of employment protection. It matters if employment protection is only assumed to be pure firing costs which are sunk costs in the case of a dismissal, if the proceeds are used to finance other labour market institutions or if the payment is directly transferred to the dismissed worker himself. It also depends on the judicial system. It matters if firms are able to anticipate their payments or if insecurity is involved. We can only give one clear answer that has already been given: In general, employment protection decreases the number of dismissals, but at the same time, decreases the incentive for job creation. Hence, the effect on unemployment stays ambiguous. However, this work has been helpful in finding out which are important issues to be considered and how the recent policy proposals can be evaluated from a theoretical point of view.

Nevertheless, further research concerning these issues is certainly necessary. In addition, we have to point out that our analysis has hardly addressed the question of a socially optimal design of employment protection. Our focus was on the effects of dismissal protection on unemployment. It is certainly of great importance to find out what is the right way to employ and the right level of employment protection. A thorough normative analysis concerning this question is definitely needed.

Appendix A

Mathematical Appendix

A.1 Nash Wage Bargaining

This section calculates wages for chapter 4. However, the calculations of the sector-specific wages of chapter 6 are in perfect analogy (for $b = t = 0$ and $\delta > 0$) and are, therefore, not repeated in an additional appendix. Maximising equation (4.8) with respect to $w(\epsilon)$ yields the following first order condition:

$$\begin{aligned} & \beta \left(W(\epsilon) - U\right)^{\beta-1} \left(J(\epsilon) + T\right)^{1-\beta} \frac{\partial W(\epsilon)}{\partial w(\epsilon)} \\ = \quad & -(1-\beta)\left(W(\epsilon) - U\right)^{\beta} \left(J(\epsilon) + T\right)^{-\beta} \frac{\partial J(\epsilon)}{\partial w(\epsilon)} \end{aligned} \tag{A.1}$$

We know from equations (4.1) and (4.6) that $\frac{\partial W(\epsilon)}{\partial w(\epsilon)} = -\frac{\partial J(\epsilon)}{\partial w(\epsilon)} = \frac{1}{r+\lambda}$. This yields the sharing rule, equation (4.10).

Inserting equations (4.1) and (4.6) into the sharing rule, equation (4.10), we obtain

$$\begin{aligned} & (1-\beta)\left(w(\epsilon) + \lambda\left(\int_{\epsilon_d}^{\epsilon_u} W(z)dG(z) + G(\epsilon_d)U\right) - (r+\lambda)U\right) \\ & = \beta\left(\epsilon - w(\epsilon) - t + \lambda\left(\int_{\epsilon_d}^{\epsilon_u} J(z)dG(z) + G(\epsilon_d)(-T)\right) + (r+\lambda)T\right). \end{aligned}$$

Solving for $w(\epsilon)$ and using the sharing rule, equation (4.10), to eliminate the integrals yields

$$w(\epsilon) = \beta(\epsilon - t + rT) + (1-\beta)rU = rU + \beta(\epsilon - t + rT - rU). \tag{A.2}$$

If workers and firms bargain for the first time, the fall-back position of firms is $V = 0$. Using (4.4), we can re-write equation (4.11) to[1]

$$\left(W^0 - U\right) = \frac{\beta}{1-\beta}\frac{c}{q(\theta)}. \tag{A.3}$$

Substituting equation (A.3) into equation (4.5) yields

$$rU = b + \theta q(\theta)\frac{\beta}{1-\beta}\frac{c}{q(\theta)} = b + \frac{\beta}{1-\beta}\theta c. \tag{A.4}$$

Inserting equation (A.4) into (A.2) yields the wage equation (4.12). Analogously, we are able to derive the wage equation for the initial wage, equation (4.13), by using equations (4.2), (4.7) and (4.9), and by maximising with respect to w^0.

A.2 Job Destruction and Job Creation Conditions for Individualized Wage Bargaining

Note again that calculations are done for chapter 4. However, calculations for chapter 6 are in perfect analogy (for $b = t = 0$ and $\delta > 0$). Substituting the wage equation (4.12) into equation (4.1) yields

$$(r+\lambda)J(\epsilon) = (1-\beta)(\epsilon-t-b)-\beta(c\theta+rT)+\lambda\left(\int_{\epsilon_d}^{\epsilon_u} J(z)dG(z) - G(\epsilon_d)T\right). \tag{A.5}$$

We can also write the firm value as

$$(r+\lambda)\left(J(\epsilon) - J(\epsilon_d)\right) = (1-\beta)(\epsilon - \epsilon_d).$$

As we know that $J(\epsilon_d) = -T$, this yields

$$J(\epsilon) = \frac{(1-\beta)(\epsilon-\epsilon_d)}{r+\lambda} - T. \tag{A.6}$$

Using equation (A.6) and $J(\epsilon_d) = -T$ to evaluate equation (A.5) at reservation productivity ϵ_d, we get

$$\begin{aligned}(r+\lambda)J(\epsilon_d) = -(r+\lambda)T &= (1-\beta)(\epsilon_d - t - b) - \beta(c\theta + rT)\\ &+ \frac{\lambda(1-\beta)}{r+\lambda}\int_{\epsilon_d}^{\epsilon_u}(z-\epsilon_d)dG(z) - \lambda T\end{aligned}$$

[1]Note that equation (A.3) is used for the education decision in chapter 6.

which yields equation (4.14).

To calculate the present discounted value of a newly created job, we combine equation (4.2), (4.13) and $J(\epsilon_d) = -T$ which gives

$$(r+\lambda)\left(J^0+T\right) = (1-\beta)(\epsilon_u - \epsilon_d) + \beta(r+\lambda)T$$

which, finally, in combination with equation (4.4), yields equation (4.15).

A.3 Basic Effects of Changes in Employment Taxes and Dismissal Taxes

Rearranging equations (4.18) and (4.19) by putting the political parameters dt and dT to the right hand side, while putting the endogenous variables $d\epsilon_d$ and $d\theta$ to the left hand side we rewrite the equations as

$$\underbrace{\begin{pmatrix} -\frac{1}{r+\lambda}\left(r+\lambda G(\epsilon_d)\right) & \frac{\beta c}{1-\beta} \\ -\frac{(1-\beta)}{r+\lambda} & \frac{cq'(\theta)}{q(\theta)^2} \end{pmatrix}}_{=B} \begin{pmatrix} d\epsilon_d \\ d\theta \end{pmatrix} = \begin{pmatrix} -1 & r \\ 0 & 1-\beta \end{pmatrix} \begin{pmatrix} dt \\ dT \end{pmatrix}. \tag{A.7}$$

With $D = det(B)$, rearranging (A.7) yields

$$\begin{pmatrix} d\epsilon_d \\ d\theta \end{pmatrix} = \frac{1}{D} \begin{pmatrix} \frac{cq'(\theta)}{q(\theta)^2} & -\frac{\beta c}{1-\beta} \\ \frac{(1-\beta)}{r+\lambda} & -\frac{1}{r+\lambda}\left(r+\lambda G(\epsilon_d)\right) \end{pmatrix} \begin{pmatrix} -1 & r \\ 0 & 1-\beta \end{pmatrix} \begin{pmatrix} dt \\ dT \end{pmatrix}$$

which leads to equations (4.21) and (4.22).

A.4 Total Effects of Changes in Employment Taxes and Dismissal Taxes

Inserting the change in employment taxes t caused by a change in dismissal taxes T, equation (4.25), into equations (4.18) and (4.19) yields after rearranging

$$\underbrace{\begin{pmatrix} -\frac{1}{r+\lambda}\left(r+\lambda G(\epsilon_d)\right) + \lambda g(\epsilon_d)\left(\frac{b}{\theta q(\theta)} - T\right) & \frac{\beta c}{1-\beta} - b\frac{\lambda G(\epsilon_d) q(\theta)(1-\eta(\theta))}{[\theta q(\theta)]^2} \\ -\frac{(1-\beta)}{r+\lambda} & \frac{cq'(\theta)}{q(\theta)^2} \end{pmatrix}}_{C}$$

$$\times \begin{pmatrix} d\epsilon_d \\ d\theta \end{pmatrix} = \begin{pmatrix} r + \lambda G(\epsilon_d) \\ 1 - \beta \end{pmatrix} dT. \tag{A.8}$$

Inverting C and solving equation (A.8) for the vector $\begin{pmatrix} d\epsilon_d \\ d\theta \end{pmatrix}$ yields

$$\begin{aligned} \begin{pmatrix} d\epsilon_d \\ d\theta \end{pmatrix} &= \frac{1}{Q} \begin{pmatrix} \frac{cq'(\theta)}{q(\theta)^2} & -\frac{\beta c}{(1-\beta)} + b\frac{\lambda G(\epsilon_d)q(\theta)(1-\eta(\theta))}{[\theta q(\theta)]^2} \\ \frac{(1-\beta)}{r+\lambda} & -\frac{1}{r+\lambda}\left(r + \lambda G(\epsilon_d)\right) + \lambda g(\epsilon_d)\left(\frac{b}{\theta q(\theta)} - T\right) \end{pmatrix} \\ &\times \begin{pmatrix} r + \lambda G(\epsilon_d) \\ 1 - \beta \end{pmatrix} dT \end{aligned}$$

which equals

$$\begin{pmatrix} d\epsilon_d \\ d\theta \end{pmatrix} = \frac{1}{Q} \begin{pmatrix} \frac{cq'(\theta)}{q(\theta)^2}\left(r + \lambda G(\epsilon_d)\right) - \beta c + (1-\beta)b\frac{\lambda G(\epsilon_d)q(\theta)(1-\eta(\theta))}{[\theta q(\theta)]^2} \\ (1-\beta)\lambda g(\epsilon_d)\left(\frac{b}{\theta q(\theta)} - T\right) \end{pmatrix} dT,$$

where $Q = det(C)$.

A.5 Sign of Determinant Q

It is possible to demonstrate that $Q > 0$ as long as an increase in employment taxes leads to an increase in the surplus of the budget for unemployment insurance. According to the budget constraint, equation (4.17), the surplus of the budget for unemployment insurance A is defined as

$$A = (1-u)\left(t + \lambda G(\epsilon_d)T\right) - bu. \tag{A.9}$$

Totally differentiating A with respect to employment taxes t yields

$$\frac{dA}{dt} = (1-u) - \left(t + \lambda G(\epsilon_d)T + b\right)\frac{du}{dt} + (1-u)\lambda g(\epsilon_d)T\frac{d\epsilon_d}{dt}.$$

Inserting the employment taxes t derived from equation (A.9) yields

$$\frac{dA}{dt} = (1-u) - \left(\frac{A+b}{1-u}\right)\frac{du}{dt} + (1-u)\lambda g(\epsilon_d)T\frac{d\epsilon_d}{dt}.$$

Considering $(1-u) = \frac{\theta q(\theta)}{\lambda G(\epsilon_d)+\theta q(\theta)}$ and partly inserting equation (4.24) for $\frac{du}{dt}$, we rewrite the last expression as

$$\begin{aligned}\frac{dA}{dt} &= (1-u)\left[1+\lambda g(\epsilon_d)\left(T-\frac{b}{\theta q(\theta)}\right)\frac{d\epsilon_d}{dt}\right. \\ &\quad \left.+\frac{\lambda G(\epsilon_d)q(\theta)(1-\eta(\theta))b}{(\theta q(\theta))^2}\frac{d\theta}{dt}\right]-\frac{A}{1-u}\frac{du}{dt}.\end{aligned}$$

When employment taxes are changed, the corresponding changes in reservation productivity and market tightness are given by equations (4.21) and (4.22) as $\frac{d\epsilon_d}{dt} = -\frac{1}{D}\frac{cq'(\theta)}{q(\theta)^2}$ and $\frac{d\theta}{dt} = -\frac{1}{D}\frac{1-\beta}{r+\lambda}$. Therefore,

$$\begin{aligned}\frac{dA}{dt} &= \frac{1-u}{D}\left[D+\lambda g(\epsilon_d)\left(\frac{b}{\theta q(\theta)}-T\right)\frac{cq'(\theta)}{q(\theta)^2}\right. \\ &\quad \left.-b\frac{\lambda G(\epsilon_d)q(\theta)(1-\eta(\theta))}{(\theta q(\theta))^2}\frac{1-\beta}{r+\lambda}\right]-\frac{A}{1-u}\frac{du}{dt} \\ &= \frac{1-u}{D}Q-\frac{A}{1-u}\frac{du}{dt}. \qquad \text{(A.10)}\end{aligned}$$

If, as postulated in the model, the budget for unemployment insurance is balanced in steady state ($A = 0$), the sign of Q is the same as the sign of $\frac{dA}{dt}$. Therefore, as long as an increase in employment taxes t leads to a surplus of the budget of unemployment insurance in steady state, the sign of Q is positive.

A.6 Job Destruction and Job Creation with a Non-Shirking Wage

To calculate reservation productivity and market tightness, the values of continuing and newly created jobs have to be calculated. Substituting the non-shirking wage, equation (5.4), into equation (5.5) yields

$$\begin{aligned}(r+\lambda)J(\epsilon) &= \bar{e}\epsilon-[(r+\lambda G(\epsilon_d)+\theta q(\theta)]\left[\frac{\bar{e}}{q}+mS\right]-\bar{e} \\ &\quad -\lambda G(\epsilon_d)T+\lambda\left[\int_{\epsilon_d}^{\epsilon_u}J(x)dG(x)\right]. \qquad \text{(A.11)}\end{aligned}$$

Therefore, the firm value can be calculated from

$$(r+\lambda)\left[J(\epsilon)-J(\epsilon_d)\right] = (\epsilon-\epsilon_d)\bar{e}$$

as

$$J(\epsilon) = \frac{(\epsilon - \epsilon_d)\bar{e}}{(r+\lambda)} - (T + zS). \tag{A.12}$$

Using equation (A.12) and the condition $J(\epsilon_d) = -(T + zS)$ to evaluate equation (A.11) at the reservation productivity yields

$$\begin{aligned}(r+\lambda)J(\epsilon_d) &= -(r+\lambda)(T+zS)\\ &= \bar{e}\epsilon_d - [(r + \lambda G(\epsilon_d) + \theta q(\theta)] \left[\frac{\bar{e}}{q} + mS\right] - \bar{e} - \lambda G(\epsilon_d)T\\ &-\lambda(1 - G(\epsilon_d))(T + zS) + \lambda \frac{\bar{e}}{(r+\lambda)} \int_{\epsilon_d}^{\epsilon_u} (x - \epsilon_d) dG(x)\end{aligned}$$

which can be transformed into equation (5.8).

To calculate the present discounted value of a newly created job, we substitute ϵ by ϵ_u in equation (A.12) and use equation (5.7) which yields equation (5.9).

A.7 Effects on Reservation Productivity and Market Tightness

We totally differentiate equations (5.8) and (5.9) with respect to θ, ϵ_d, m, z, S and T. This yields

$$\begin{aligned}&\left\{\frac{\bar{e}}{r+\lambda}(r + \lambda G(\epsilon_d)) - \lambda g(\epsilon_d)\left[\frac{\bar{e}}{q} + (m-z)S\right]\right\} d\epsilon_d\\ &- \left[\frac{\bar{e}}{q} + mS\right][\theta q(\theta)]' \, d\theta = (r + \lambda G(\epsilon_d) + \theta q(\theta))Sdm\\ &-(r + \lambda G(\epsilon_d))Sdz + [m(r + \lambda G(\epsilon_d) + \theta q(\theta))\\ &-(r + \lambda G(\epsilon_d))z]dS - rdT\end{aligned} \tag{A.13}$$

for equation (5.8) and

$$-\frac{\bar{e}}{r+\lambda} d\epsilon_d + \frac{cq'(\theta)}{q(\theta)^2} d\theta = Sdz + zdS + dT \tag{A.14}$$

for equation (5.9). Writing the system of equations (A.13) and (A.14) as a matrix and following Appendix A.3 yields equations (5.14) to (5.19).

A.8 Difference of the Sector-specific Change of Reservation Productivity

Employed high-skilled workers obtain more benefits from employment protection if reservation productivity of high-skilled workers falls by more than the one for low-skilled workers when employment protection is increased ($\frac{d\epsilon_d^s}{dT} < \frac{d\epsilon_d^l}{dT}$). Totally differentiating the JD and JC, equations (6.8) and (6.9), yield

$$\frac{d\epsilon_d^i}{dT} = -\frac{(r+\delta+\lambda)(r+\delta)cq'(\theta^i) - q(\theta^i)^2\beta c}{(r+\delta+\lambda G(\epsilon_d^i))cq'(\theta^i) - q(\theta^i)^2\beta c}. \tag{A.15}$$

The above condition ($\frac{d\epsilon_d^s}{dT} < \frac{d\epsilon_d^l}{dT}$) yields

$$\begin{aligned} &\lambda\left(G(\epsilon_d^s) - G(\epsilon_d^l)\right) \\ &< \frac{\beta}{\bar{\eta}}\left(\frac{(r+\delta+\lambda)(r+\delta) + (r+\delta+\lambda G(\epsilon_d^l))}{(r+\delta+\lambda)(r+\delta)}\theta^s q(\theta^s)\right. \\ &\left. -\frac{(r+\delta+\lambda)(r+\delta) + (r+\delta+\lambda G(\epsilon_d^s))}{(r+\delta+\lambda)(r+\delta)}\theta^l q(\theta^l)\right), \end{aligned} \tag{A.16}$$

where $0 < \bar{\eta} = -\frac{q'(\theta^l)}{q(\theta^l)}\theta^l = -\frac{q'(\theta^s)}{q(\theta^s)}\theta^s < 1$ for a Cobb-Douglas matching function.

Since $\epsilon_d^s < \epsilon_d^l$ and $\theta^s > \theta^l$, as shown above, the left hand side in equation (A.16) is smaller than zero, while the right hand side is larger. This means employed, high-skilled workers benefit more from the same change of the level of employment protection than employed low-skilled workers.

This is due to the fact that when changing employment protection, the original levels of reservation productivity and market tightness differ in both sectors due to the productivity difference. The higher the productivity difference a^s, the more beneficial the effect of increasing employment protection for the employed high-skilled compared to the employed low-skilled workers.

A.9 Calculating the Threshold for the Bargaining Power of Workers

Combining the changes of market tightness due to a change in employment protection for $\frac{d\theta^l}{dT} < \frac{d\theta^s}{dT}$, according to equation (6.14) yields

$$\begin{aligned} &\frac{(1-\beta)\lambda G(\epsilon_d^l)}{(r+\delta+\lambda G(\epsilon_d^l))\frac{c}{q(\theta^l)^2}q'(\theta^l)-\beta c} \\ &< \frac{(1-\beta)\lambda G(\epsilon_d^s)}{(r+\delta+\lambda G(\epsilon_d^s))\frac{c}{q(\theta^s)^2}q'(\theta^s)-\beta c}. \end{aligned} \tag{A.17}$$

After multiplying by c, equation (A.17) can be rewritten to

$$\begin{aligned} &G(\epsilon_d^l)\left((r+\delta+\lambda G(\epsilon_d^s))\frac{q'(\theta^s)}{q(\theta^s)^2}-\beta\right) \\ &< G(\epsilon_d^s)\left((r+\delta+\lambda G(\epsilon_d^l))\frac{q'(\theta^l)}{q(\theta^l)^2}-\beta\right), \end{aligned}$$

which after adding $\beta G(\epsilon_d^s)$ and dividing by $G(\epsilon_d^s)((r+\delta+\lambda G(\epsilon_d^l))$ and $\frac{q'(\theta^s)}{q(\theta^s)^2}$ yields

$$\frac{G(\epsilon_d^l)}{G(\epsilon_d^s)}\frac{(r+\delta+\lambda G(\epsilon_d^s))}{(r+\delta+\lambda G(\epsilon_d^l))}-\beta\frac{G(\epsilon_d^l)-G(\epsilon_d^s)}{G(\epsilon_d^s)(r+\delta+\lambda G(\epsilon_d^s))}\frac{q(\theta^s)^2}{q'(\theta^s)} > \frac{\frac{q'(\theta^l)}{q(\theta^l)^2}}{\frac{q'(\theta^s)}{q(\theta^s)^2}}. \tag{A.18}$$

Enhancing (A.18) with $(\frac{\theta^l}{\theta^l})/(\frac{\theta^s}{\theta^s}) = 1$ and switching $\theta^i q(\theta^i)$ from the right hand side to the left hand side and some rearranging yields

$$\left(\frac{G(\epsilon_d^l)}{G(\epsilon_d^s)}\frac{(r+\delta+\lambda G(\epsilon_d^s))}{(r+\delta+\lambda G(\epsilon_d^l))}-\beta\frac{G(\epsilon_d^l)-G(\epsilon_d^s)}{G(\epsilon_d^s)(r+\delta+\lambda G(\epsilon_d^s))}\frac{q(\theta^s)^2}{q'(\theta^s)}\right)\frac{\theta^l q(\theta^l)}{\theta^s q(\theta^s)} > \frac{\eta^l}{\eta^s}. \tag{A.19}$$

Note that $\eta^i = -\frac{q'(\theta^i)}{\theta^i q(\theta^i)}$ and $\eta^l = \eta^s = \bar{\eta}$ for a Cobb-Douglas matching function as assumed (also see Pissarides 2000, chapter 8) and, hence, $\eta^l/\eta^s = 1$. Now multiplying with $\theta^s/\theta^s = 1$ and substituting η^s yields equation (6.15).

A.10 Maximising Firm's Profits in a Unionised Economy

The first order conditions for the maximisation problem of equations (7.1) and (7.2) are given by

$$e^{-rt}c + q(\theta)\mu = 0 \tag{A.20}$$

and

$$e^{-rt}\left[F'(n_i) - w_i - \lambda(1+\gamma)T\right] - \lambda\mu + \dot{\mu} = 0. \tag{A.21}$$

From equation (A.20) we see that $\mu = e^{-rt}\frac{c}{q(\theta)}$. Using this, we know that $\dot{\mu} = -re^{-rt}\frac{c}{q(\theta)}$. Substituting μ and $\dot{\mu}$ into equation (A.21) yields equation (7.3).

A.11 Wage Bargaining in a Unionised Economy

Maximising equation (7.6) with respect to w_i and n_i subject to equation (7.3) yields

$$n_i \frac{\partial W_i}{\partial w_i} - \mu = 0 \tag{A.22}$$

and

$$(W_i - U) + \mu F''(n_i) = 0. \tag{A.23}$$

From equation (A.22) we see that $\mu = n_i \frac{\partial W_i}{\partial w_i}$. Further, we know from equation (7.5) that $\frac{\partial W_i}{\partial w_i} = \frac{1}{r+\lambda}$. Substituting this into equation (A.23), using equation (7.5) and some rearranging yields equation (7.7).

A.12 Effects of Increasing Employment Protection in a Unionised Economy

After totally differentiating equations (7.11) and (7.9) with respect to n, θ and T, we get

$$\left\{F''(n) + \frac{r+\lambda+\theta q(\theta)}{r+\lambda}\left[F''(n) + nF'''(n)\right]\right\} dn$$

$$+\left\{(r+\lambda)\frac{cq'(\theta)}{q(\theta)^2} + \frac{nF''(n)q(\theta)(1-\eta(\theta))}{r+\lambda}\right\} d\theta = \lambda dT \qquad \text{(A.24)}$$

for equation (7.11) and

$$-dn + \frac{q(\theta)[1-\eta(\theta)]\lambda}{(\lambda+\theta q(\theta))^2} d\theta = 0 \qquad \text{(A.25)}$$

for equation (7.9). Writting equations (A.24) and (A.25) in matrix form and following Appendix A.3, we get equations (7.15) and (7.16).

Bibliography

[1] Acemoglu, D. and R. Shimer (1997), Efficient Wage Dispersion. CEPR Discussion Paper, No. 1572.

[2] Addison, J. T. (1989), Job Rights and Economic Dislocation. Microeconomic Issues in Labour Economics, R. Drago and R. Perlman (eds.), New York, pp. 130-154.

[3] Addison, J. T. and P. Teixeira (2003), The Economics of Employment Protection. Journal of Labor Research 24, pp. 85-129.

[4] Agell, J. (2002), On the Determinants of Labour Market Institutions: Rent Seeking vs. Social Insurance. German Economic Review 3, 107-135.

[5] Albrecht, J. and S. Vroman (2005), Equilibrium Search with Time-Varying Unemployment Benefits. Economic Journal 115, pp. 631-648.

[6] Alchian, A. A. (1969), Information Costs, Pricing and Resource Unemployment. Western Economic Journal 7, pp. 109-128.

[7] Alvarez, F. and M. Veracierto (2000), Labor-Market Policies in an Equilibrium Search Model. NBER Macroeconomics Annual 1999, B. Bernanke and J. J. Rotemberg (eds.), MIT Press, Cambridge, pp. 265-314.

[8] Anderson P. and B. Meyer (2000), The Effects of the Unemployment Insurance Payroll Tax on Wages, Employment, Claims and Denials. Journal of Public Economics 78, pp. 81-106.

[9] Atkinson, A. B. and J. Micklewright (1991), Unemployment Compensation and Labor Market Transitions: A Critical Review. Journal of Economic Literature 29, pp. 1679-1727.

[10] Baker, D., A. Glyn, D. Howell and J. Schmitt (2005), Labour Market Institutions and Unemployment: A Critical Assessment of Cross-Country Evidence. Fighting Unemployment. The Limits of Free Market Orthodoxy, D. R. Howell (edt.), Oxford University Press, New York, pp. 72-118.

[11] Baumann, F. (2006), Efficiency Wages and Severance Payments with Endogenous Shocks. Manuscript, Johannes Gutenberg-University of Mainz, mimeo.

[12] Baumann, F. and N. Stähler (2006), Financing Unemployment Benefits: Dismissal versus Employment Taxes. Labour 20, 433-451.

[13] Bean, C. R. (1997), Comment to: Exploring the Political Economy of Labour Market Institutions by Gilles Saint-Paul. Economic Policy 23, pp. 265 - 292.

[14] Behaghel, L., B. Crépon and B. Sédillot (2005), The Perverse Effects of Partial Employment Protection Reform: Experience Rating and French Older Workers. IZA Discussion Paper, No. 1679.

[15] Belot, M. and J. C. van Ours (2002), Welfare Effects of Employment Protection. CEPR Discussion Paper, No. 3396.

[16] Belot, M. and J. C. van Ours (2004), Does the recent success of some OECD countries in lowering their unemployment rates lie in the clever design of their labour market reforms? Oxford Economic Papers 56, pp. 621-642.

[17] Bentolila, S. and G. Bertola (1990), Firing Costs and Labor Demand: How Bad is Eurosclerosis? Review of Economic Studies 57, pp. 381-402.

[18] Berger, H. (1998), Regulation in Germany: Some Stylized Facts About Its Time Path, Causes and Consequences. Zeitschrift für Wirtschafts- und Sozialwissenschaften 118, pp. 185-220.

[19] Bertola, G. (1990), Job Security, Employment and Wages. European Economic Review, Vol. 34, pp. 851-886.

[20] Bertola, G. (1992), Labor Turnover Costs and Average Labor Demand. Journal of Economics 10, pp. 389-411.

[21] Bertola, G. (1999), Microeconomic Perspectives on Aggregated Labor Markets. Handbook of Labor Economics, O. Ashenfelter and D. Card (eds.), Vol. 3C, Elsevier, Amsterdam, pp. 2985-3028.

[22] Bertola, G., T. Boeri and S. Cazes (1999), Employment Protection and Labour Market Adjustment in OECD Countries: Evolving Institutions and Variable Enforcement. ILO Employment and Training Papers 48, Geneva.

[23] Bertola, G., T. Boeri and S. Cazes (2000), Employment Protection in Industrialized Countries: The Case for New Indicators. International Labour Review 139, pp. 57-72.

[24] Bertola, G., R. J. Caballero (1994), Irreversibility and Aggregated Investment. Review of Economic Studies 61, pp. 223-246.

[25] Blanchard, O. (2006), European Unemployment. Economic Policy January 2006, pp. 5-59.

[26] Blanchard, O. and P. A. Diamond (1990), The Cyclical Behavior of the Gross Flows of U.S. Workers. Brookings Papers on Economic Activity 2, pp. 85-155.

[27] Blanchard, O. and P. Portugal (2001), What Hides Behind an Unemployment Rate: Comparing Portuguese and U.S. Labor Markets. American Economic Review 91, pp. 187-207.

[28] Blanchard, O. and J. Tirole (2004), The Optimal Design of Unemployment Insurance and Employment Protection. A First Pass. NBER Working Paper, No. 10443.

[29] Blanchflower, D. G. and S. M. Burges (1996), Job Creation and Job Destruction in Great Britain in the 1980s. Industrial and Labor Relations Review 50, pp. 17-38.

[30] Blau, F. D. and L. M. Kahn (1999), Institutions and Laws in the Labor Market. Handbook of Labor Economics, O. Ashenfelter and D. Card (eds.), Vol. 3A, Elsevier, Amsterdam, pp. 1399-1461.

[31] Bliss, C. J. and N. H. Stern (1978), Productivity, Wages and Nutrition, Part II: Some Observations. Journal of Development Economics 5, pp. 363-398.

[32] Boeri, T., J. I. Conde-Ruiz, and V. Galasso (2004), Cross-skill Redistribution and the Tradeoff between Unemployment Benefits and Employment Protection. IZA Discussion Paper, No. 1371.

[33] Booth, A. and M. Chatterji (1989), Redundancy Payments and Firm-Specific Training. Economica 56, pp. 505-521.

[34] Booth, A. (1995a), The Economics of the Trade Union. Cambridge University Press, Cambridge.

[35] Booth, A. (1995b), Layoffs with Payoffs: A Bargaining Model of Union Wages and Severance Pay Determination. Economica 62, pp. 551-564.

[36] Bovenberg, A. (2003), Tax Policy and Labor Market Performance. CESifo Working Paper, No. 1035.

[37] Broersma, L. and J. C. van Ours (1999), Job Searchers, Job Matches and the Elasticity of Matching. Labour Economics 6, pp. 77-93.

[38] Büchtemann, C. F. (1993), Introduction: Employment Security and Labor Markets. Employment Security and Labor Market Behavior. Interdisciplinary Approaches and International Evidence, C. F. Büchtemann (edt.), Ithaca, New York, pp. 3-66.

[39] Burda, M. (1992), A Note on Firing Costs and Severance Benefits in Equilibrium Unemployment. Scandinavian Journal of Economics 39, pp. 479-489.

[40] Burda, M. (2003), Humankapital und Arbeitsmarktinstitutionen bei gleichgewichtiger Arbeitslosigkeit. Bildung - Wirtschaftswissenschaftliches Seminar Ottobeuren, W.

Franz, H. J. Ramser and M. Stadler (eds.), Vol. 33, Mohr Siebeck, Tübingen, pp. 119-140.

[41] Burdett, K. and R. Wright (1989), Optimal Firm Size, Taxes, and Unemployment. Journal of Public Economics 39, pp. 275-287.

[42] Burgert, Derik (2006), The Impact of German Job Protection Legislation on Job Creation in Small Establishments. Applied Economics Quarterly 52, pp. 123-139.

[43] Buttler, F. and U. Walwei (1990), Effizienzwirkungen des Kündigungsschutzes. Mitteilungen aus der Arbeitsmarkt- und Berufsforschung 23, pp. 386-393.

[44] Caballero, R. J. and M. L. Hammour (1994), The Cleansing Effect of Recessions. American Economic Review 84, pp. 1350-1368.

[45] Cahuc. P. and E. Lehmann (2000), Should Unemployment Benefits Decrease with the Unemployment Spell? Journal of Public Economics 77, pp. 135-153.

[46] Cahuc. P. and F. Malherbet (2004), Unemployment Compensation Finance and Labor Market Rigidity. Journal of Public Economics 88, pp. 481-501.

[47] Cahuc. P. and A. Zylberberg (2005), Optimum Income Taxation and Layoff Taxes. IZA Discussion Paper, No. 1678.

[48] Carter, T. J. (1992), Labor Subsidies and Just-Cause Employment Laws in an Efficiency Wage Model. Southern Economic Journal 59, pp. 49-57.

[49] Cartter, A. M. (1959), Theory of Wages and Employment. Homewoods, R. D. Irvin (edt)., Illinios.

[50] Charlot, O. and B. Decreuse (2005), Self-Selection in Education with Matching Frictions. Labour Economics 12, pp. 251-267.

[51] Coe, D. and D. J. Snower (1997), Policy Complementaries: The Case for Fundamental Labor Market Reform. IMF Staff Papers 44, pp. 1-35.

[52] Cole, H. L. and R. Rogerson (1996), Can the Mortensen-Pissarides Matching Model Match the Business Cycle Facts? Staff Report 224. Federal Reverse Bank of Minneapolis, Research Department.

[53] Davis, S. J. and J. C. Haltiwanger (1990), Gross Job Creation and Destruction: Microeconomic Evidence and Macroeconomic Implications. NBER Macroeconomic Annual 5, pp. 123-168.

[54] Davis, S. J. and J. C. Haltiwanger (1992), Gross Job Creation, Gross Job Destruction, and Employment Reallocation. Quarterly Journal of Economics 107, pp. 819-863.

[55] Di Tella, R. and R. MacCulloch (2005), The Consequences of Labor Market Flexibility: Panel Evidence Based on Survey Data. European Economic Review 49, pp. 1225-1259.

[56] Dolado, J. C. Garcis-Serrano and J. F. Jimeno] (2002), Drawing Lessons from the Boom of Temporary Jobs in Spain. Economic Journal 112, pp. 270-295.

[57] Dolado, J., M. Jansen and J. F. Jimeno-Serrano (2005), Dual Employment Protection Legislation: A Framework for Analysis. CEPR Discussion Paper, No. 5033.

[58] Dunlop, J. T. (1944), Wage Determination under Trade Unions. Reprints of Economic Classics (1966), A. M. Kelley (edt.), New York.

[59] Ellguth, P. and S. Kohaut (2005), Tarifbindung und betriebliche Interessenvertretung. Aktuelle Forschungsergebnisse aus dem IAB-Betriebspanel. WSI Mitteilungen 7, pp. 398-403.

[60] European Commission (2004), Employment in Europe. Luxemburg.

[61] Fath, J. and C. Fuest (2005a), Temporary Layoffs and Unemployment Insurance: Is Experience Rating Desirable? German Economic Review 6, pp. 471-483.

[62] Fath, J. and C. Fuest (2005b), Experience Rating and Unemployment Insurance in the USA: A Model for Europe? CESifo DICE Report, No. 2/2005, pp. 45-50.

[63] Fath, J. and C. Fuest (2005c), Experience Rating versus Employment Protection Laws in a Model where Firms Monitor Workers. Scandinavian Journal of Economics 107, pp. 299-313.

[64] Feldstein, M. S. (1976), Temporary Layoffs in the Theory of Unemployment. Journal of Political Economy 84, pp. 937-957.

[65] Fella, G. (2000), Efficiency Wage and Efficient Redundancy Pay. European Economic Review 44, pp. 1473-1490.

[66] Fella, G. (2005), Termination Restrictions and Investment in General Training. European Economic Review, Vol. 49, pp. 1479-1499.

[67] Fellner, W. (1947), Prices and Wages under Bilateral Monopoly. Quarterly Journal of Economics 61, pp. 503-532.

[68] Fredriksson, P. and B. Holmlund (2001), Optimal Unemployment Insurance in Search Equilibrium. Journal of Labor Economics 19, pp. 370-399.

[69] Galdón-Sánches, J. E. and M. Güell (2000), Let's Go To Court! Firing Costs and Dismissal Conflicts. Princeton University, Industrial Relations Section, Working Paper, No. 444.

[70] Galdón-Sánches, J. E. and M. Güell (2003), Dismissal Conflicts and Unemployment. European Economic Review 47, pp. 323-335.

[71] Garibaldi, P. (1998), Job Flow Dynamics and Firing Restrictions. European Economic Review 42, pp. 245-275.

[72] Garibaldi, P. (2004), Search Unemployment with Advanced Notice. Macroeconomic Dynamics 8, pp. 51-75.

[73] Garibaldi, P. and L. G. Violante (2002), Firing Tax and Severance Payments in Search Economies: A Comparison. CEPR Discussion paper, No. 3636.

[74] Garibaldi, P. and L. G. Violante (2005), The Employment Effects of Severance Payments with Wage Rigidities. The Economic Journal 115, pp. 799-832.

[75] German Council of Economic Experts (2003), Staatsfinanzen konsolidieren - Steuersystem reformieren. Reutlingen: Elsevier Group.

[76] German Council of Economic Experts (2005), Die Chance nutzen - Reformen mutig voranbringen. Reutlingen: Elsevier Group.

[77] German Council of Economic Experts (2006), Widerstreitende Interessen - Ungenutzte Chancen. Reutlingen: Elsevier Group.

[78] Goerke, L. (2002a), Taxes and Unemployment. Kluwer Academic Publishers, Bosten, Dodrecht and London.

[79] Goerke, L. (2002b), On Dismissal Pay. Labour Economics 9, pp. 497-512.

[80] Goerke, L. and M. Pannenberg (2004), Berufliche Weiterbildung "on-the-job" und Auflösung von Beschäftigungsverhältnissen. DFG Research Group 'Heterogeneous Labour', Discussion Paper, No. 04/22.

[81] Grubb, D. and W. Wells (1993), Employment Regulation and Patterns of Work in EC Countries. OECD Economic Studies 21, pp. 7-58.

[82] Guelfi, A. (2004), Employment Protection and the Incidence of Unemployment: A Theoretical Framework. Labour, Vol. 18, pp. 29-52.

[83] Güell, M. (1999), Employment Protection and Unemployment in an Efficiency Wage Model. Princeton University, Industrial Relations Section, Working Paper, No. 432.

[84] Hansen, C. T. (1999), Lower Tax Progression, Longer Hours and Higher Wages. Scandinavian Journal of Economics 101, pp. 49-65.

[85] Hopenhayn, H. and J. P. Nicolini (1997), Optimal Unemployment Insurance. Journal of Political Economy 105, pp. 412-438.

[86] Hopenhayn, H. and R. Rogerson (1993), Job Turnover and Policy Evaluation: A General Equilibrium Analysis. Journal of Political Economy 101, pp. 915-938.

[87] Hosios, A. J. (1990), On the Efficiency of Matching and Related Models of Search Unemployment. Review of Economic Studies, Vol. 57, pp. 279-298.

[88] Howell, D.R. and F. Huebler (2005), Wage Compression and the Unemployment Crisis: Labor Market Institutions, Skills, and Inequality-Unemployment Tradeoffs. Fighting Unemployment. The Limits of Free Market Orthodoxy, D. R. Howell (edt.), Oxford University Press, New York, pp. 35-71.

[89] Hromadka, W. and F. Maschmann (2002), Arbeitsrecht Band 1. Individualarbeitsrecht. Second edition, Springer, Berlin.

[90] Ichino, A., M. Polo and E. Rettore (2003), Are Judges Biased by Labor Market Conditions? European Economic Review 47, pp. 913-944.

[91] Kohns, S. (2000), Different Skill Levels and Firing Costs in a Matching Model with Uncertainty - An Extension of Mortensen and Pissarides (1994). IZA Discussion Paper, No. 104.

[92] Kolm, A. and B. Larsen (2003), Social Norm, the Informal Sector, and Unemployment. FinanzArchiv, Vol. 59, pp. 407-424.

[93] Kuhns, P. (1992), Mandatory Notice. Journal of Labor Economics 10, pp. 117-137.

[94] Layard, N. and S. Nickel (1999), Labor Market Institutions and Economic Performance. Handbook of Labor Economics, O. Ashenfelter and D. Card (eds.), Vol. 3C, Elsevier, Amsterdam, pp. 3029-3083.

[95] Lazear, E. P. (1990), Job Security Provisions and Employment. Quarterly Journal of Economics 105, pp. 699-726.

[96] Leibenstein, H. (1957), The Theory of Unemployment in Backward Economies. Journal of Political Economy 65, pp. 91-103.

[97] Leontieff, W. (1946), The Annual Guaranteed Wage Contract. Journal of Political Economy 54, pp. 76-79.

[98] Levine, D. I. (1989), Just-cause Employment Policies When Unemployment is a Worker Discipline Device. American Economic Review 79, pp. 902-905.

[99] L'Haridon, O. and F. Malherbet (2003), Protection de l'Emploi et Performance du Marche du Travail. Revue Francaise d'Economie 17, pp. 21-69.

[100] Lindbeck, A. and D. J. Snower (1986), Wage Setting, Unemployment, and Insider-Outsider Relations. American Economic Review 76, pp. 235-239.

[101] Lindbeck, A. and D. J. Snower (1987), Union Activity, Unemployment Persistence and Wage Employment Ratchets. European Economic Review 31, pp. 157-167.

[102] Ljungqvist, L. and T. Sargent (1995), Welfare States and Unemployment. Economic Theory 6, pp. 143-160.

[103] Ljungqvist, L. and T. Sargent (2000), Recursive Macroeconomic Theory. Cambridge USA: MIT Press.

[104] Manning, A. (1995), Developments in Labor Market Theory and their Implications for Macroeconomic Policy. Scottish Journal of Political Economy 42, pp. 250-266.

[105] Marceau, N. (1993), Unemployment Insurance and Market Structure. Journal of Public Economics 52, pp. 237-249.

[106] McDonald, I. M. and R. M. Solow (1981), Wage Bargaining and Employment. American Economic Review 71, pp. 896-908.

[107] Modesto, L. (2004), Unions, Firing Costs and Unemployment. IZA Discussion Paper, No. 1157.

[108] Modesto, L. and J. P. Thomas (2001), An Analysis of Labor Adjustment Costs in Unionized Economies. Labour Economics 8, pp. 475-501.

[109] Moen, E. R. (1997), Competetive Search Equilibrium. Journal of Political Economy 105, pp. 385-411.

[110] Mortensen, D. T. (1970), A Theory of Wage and Employment Dynamics. The Microeconomic Foundations of Employment and Inflation Theory, E. S. Phelps et al. (eds.), Norton, New York, pp. 847-862.

[111] Mortensen, D. T. (1977), Unemployment Insurance and Job Search Decisions. Industrial and Labor Relations Review 30, pp. 505-517.

[112] Mortensen, D. T. and C. Pissarides (1994), Job Creation and Job Destruction in the Theory of Unemployment. Review of Economic Studies 61, 397-415.

[113] Mortensen, D.T. and C. Pissarides (1999), New Developments in Models of Search in the Labor Market. Handbook of Labor Economics, O. Ashenfelter and D. Card (eds.), Vol. 3B, Elsevier, Amsterdam, pp. 2567-2627.

[114] Mortensen, D. T. and C. Pissarides (2003), Taxes, Subsidies, and Equilibrium Labour Market Outcomes. Designing Inclusion: Tools to Raise Low-End Pay and Employment in Private Enterprise, E. S. Phelps (edt.), Cambridge University Press, Cambridge, pp. 44-73.

[115] OECD (1999), Employment Outlook. Paris.

[116] OECD (2004a), Employment Outlook. Paris.

[117] OECD (2004b), Education at a Glance. Paris.

[118] Petrongolo, B. and C. Pissarides (2001), Looking into the Black Box: A Survey of the Matching Function. Journal of Economic Literature 39, pp. 390-431.

[119] Phelps, E. S. (1968), Money-Wage Dynamics and Labor-Market Equilibrium. Journal of Political Economy 76, pp. 678-711.

[120] Pindyck, R. S. and D. L. Rubinfeld (2005), Microeconomics. 6th Edition, Prentice Hall.

[121] Pissarides, C. (1998), The Impact of Employment Tax Cuts on Unemployment and Wages; The Role of Unemployment Benefits and Tax Structure. European Economic Review 42, pp. 155-183.

[122] Pissarides, C. (1999), Policy Influences on Unemployment: The European Experience. Scottish Journal of Political Economy 46, pp. 389-418.

[123] Pissarides, C. (2000), Equilibrium Unemployment Theory. 2nd Edition, Cambridge USA: MIT Press.

[124] Pissarides, C. (2001), Employment Protection. Labour Economics 8, pp. 131-159.

[125] Pita, C. (1997), Breach Penalties in Labour Contracts: Advanced Notice and Severance Pay. Labour 11, pp. 469-495.

[126] Riphahn, R. T. (2004), Employment Protection and Effort Among German Employees. Economics Letters 85, pp. 353-357.

[127] Rocheteau, G. (1999a), Balanced-Budget Rules and Indeterminancy of Equilibrium Unemployment Rate. Oxford Economic Papers 51, pp. 399-409.

[128] Rocheteau, G. (1999b), Can an Unemployment Insurance System Generate Multiple Natural Rates? International Tax and Public Finance 6, pp. 379-387.

[129] Rosen, A. and Wasmer, E. (2002), Higher Education Levels, Firm's Outside Options and the Wage Structure. CEPR Discussion paper, No. 3186.

[130] Saha, B. (1993), Implicit Contracts under Job Security Regulations. Keio Economic Studies 30, pp. 53-64.

[131] Saint-Paul, G. (1995), The High Unemployment Trap. The Quarterly Journal of Economics 110, pp. 527-550.

[132] Saltari, E. and R. Tilli (2004), Labor Market Performance and Flexibility: Which Comes First? Topics in Macroeconomics 4, pp. 1-23.

[133] Sanfey, P. J. (1995), Insiders and Outsiders in Union Models. Journal of Economic Surveys 9, pp. 255-284.

[134] Sato, Y. and H. Sugiura (2003), On Labor Policies Affecting Investment in General Human Capital. Labour 17, pp. 599-622.

[135] Scarpetta, S. (1996), Assessing the Role of Labour Market Policies and Institutional Setting on Unemployment: A Cross-Country Study. OECD, Economic Studies 26, pp. 43-98.

[136] Shapiro, C. and J. E. Stiglitz (1984), Equilibrium Unemployment as a Worker Discipline Devise. American Economic Review 74, pp. 433-444.

[137] Shi, S. and Wen, Q. (1999), Labor Market Search and the Dynamic Effects of Taxes and Subsidies. Journal of Monetary Economics 43, pp. 457-495.

[138] Südekum, J. and P. Rühmann (2003), Severance Payments and Firm-Specific Human Capital. Labour 17, pp. 47-62.

[139] Staffolani, S. (2002), Firing Costs, Efficiency Wages and Unemployment. Labour 16, pp. 803-830.

[140] Stähler, N. (2006), Employment Protection: Its Effects on Different Skill Groups and on the Incentive to Become Skilled. Jahrbücher für Nationalökonomie und Statistik 226, pp. 41-54.

[141] Stiglitz, J. E. (1976), The Efficiency Wage Hypothesis, Surplus Labour and the Distribution of Income in L.D.C.'s. Oxford Economic Papers 28, pp. 185-207.

[142] Tilli, R. (2003), Politiche del Lavoro ed Esternalita di Ricerca. Studi Economici 58, pp. 77-101.

[143] Topel, R. and F. Welch (1980), Unemployment Insurance: Survey and Extensions. Economica 47, pp. 351-379.

[144] Thurow, L. (1987), The Zero-Sum Solution. The Route to Economic Growth, Rev. Edition, Harmondsworth, GB.

[145] Walwei, U. (1996), Flexibilisierung und Regulierung des Beschäftigungssystems: Optionen und Effekte. Mitteilungen aus der Arbeitsmarkt- und Berufsforschung 29, pp. 219-227.

[146] Wang, C. and S. D. Williamson (1996), Unemployment Insurance with Moral Hazard in a Dynamic Economy. Carnegie-Rochester Conference Series on Public Policy 44, pp. 1-41.

[147] Wasmer, E. (2003), Interpreting Europe and US Labor Markets Differences: The Specificity of Human Capital Investment. CEPR Discussion Paper, No. 3780.

FSC
www.fsc.org
MIX
Papier | Fördert gute Waldnutzung
FSC® C083411

Kolibri 360 GmbH
Ferdinand-Jühlke-Straße 7
99095 Erfurt, Deutschland
produktsicherheit@kolibri360.de

Druck:
CPI Druckdienstleistungen GmbH
im Auftrag der
Kolibri 360 GmbH
Ferdinand-Jühlke-Str. 7
99095 Erfurt